A LITTLE HISTORY
OF EXMOOR

EXMOOR TODAY

A LITTLE HISTORY OF EXMOOR

by

HOPE L. BOURNE

ILLUSTRATED BY
THE AUTHOR

LONDON

J. M. DENT & SONS LTD

Made in Great Britain
at the
Aldine Press · Letchworth · Herts
for
J. M. DENT & SONS LTD
Aldine House · Bedford Street · London
First published 1968

SBN: 460 07736 8

CONTENTS

ordnance survey map. Hill farms of the eighteenth century. Ox teams. Sheep. Exmoor ponies. Pack-horses. Common rights. The farming year. Forest accounts. Disafforestation. The Acland pony herd.

Purchase of Exmoor Forest. Boundary walls and roads. Land reclamation. First crops and stock. Horses. The curse of horsemen. Frederick Knight. New farms. Simonsbath and mining ventures. New methods of farming. Sheep and Scottish shepherds. The Fortescues. Enclosure of the commons. The first carts. Tourists and holiday folk. Coaches. Lynton railway. Buses. The life of the village. Devon and Somerset Staghounds. A royal visit. Foxhounds and harriers. Exmoor ponies.

ILLUSTRATIONS

The chapter-head decorations are the head of an Exmoor Horn ram

PREFACE

Hills in the dawn, blue-grey in the morning light, long sky-lines under the breaking cloud, the murmur of distant streams in deep wet combes, the song of many birds in the leafy hedge-tops of May, the movement of sheep on the early grass: here, where I sit and look out through my window, I see the green fields of the hill farm, and hear the first sounds of the morning, while beyond the shaggy beech hedges the heather hills look back at me and wait for the fire of the rising sun. Another morning and another day, one more in the chain of life. Soon the work of the farm will begin again, the daily round of a pastoral life, little changed in its essentials from centuries past, even though the sound of a tractor has now replaced the clash of hooves in the cobbled yard.

Here is Exmoor, here are the hills high under a windy sky, here are the combes with their woods and streams, here are the farms and fields and grazing stock. Here is space and freedom, and a land where all the while one is aware of the forces of nature, sunshine and storm, both around one and within oneself. Here one can still walk and ride and hunt and know that life is good. For many years now this hill country has been my home, and I have known and loved it as no other, and have walked or ridden over every part of it, watched the deer on the heights, followed the hounds down into the deep valleys and been welcome at many a farmhouse under the hill.

To one who lives in a country, and who loves that country, and to whom each hill and valley and every feature is part of a living presence, there is ever with one a sense of depth in time as well as space, and always one is conscious of other hands and minds and forces that have like oneself lived and had being here, and who, living, have moulded and been moulded by this thing that is a land, this particular and peculiar portion of the surface of the earth which is itself and no other. As one passes by the long-crumbling stone-faced banks with the heather in their crannies, and listens to the wind in the beech-cresting above them, and looks down upon some lonely farm with its wet slate roofs shining in the rain, or raises one's eyes to the silent barrows on the rims above the oak woods, always there is with one the presence of other lives and ways, and always the wondering question, half asked and without the expectation of an answer: Who made this wall, who first set this farm half hidden in the hill against the wind, and why, and whose hands raised long ago that strange mound upon the hill top? What urges drove them, these folk whose being we touch for a moment as we see and pass these things that are of their making, and whom for the fraction of a moment we know again when the sun touches the blades of grass in the evening, and our deeper senses stir from under the ice of our intellect?

The dim light of history and the colder one of archaeology may both tell us something of all the mingled forces, natural and human, which made and moulded this land through the long-forgotten ages to bequeath it to us this day in its present form. Yet they will tell us nothing of truth or reality if they present their facts only with the dead lifelessness of a science. Life can be created and re-created only by life, and it is only by the use of imagination, which is the spirit of life, that we can perceive reality.

It is because of this that I have attempted to write the following small book. There are many I think who, like myself, love this wild moorland country and all its strong fierce character, and who loving it and being conscious of its mysteries and natural beauty would also know something of its depth in time and human endeavour if they could. Yet to date there is no simple readable history of Exmoor. There do exist a number of scholarly works (*see* Bibliography), but these are all special-ized studies of some single or particular facets of the local history. There are also numerous topographical books, but these, though they may deal adequately with the present aspect of the country, go little below the surface, as it were, and none give any consecutive sequence to the things that have made the land as it is. One may, if one is drawn to do so, wade through the innumerable stiff and dusty tomes which comprise the transactions of the Devonshire Association and the proceedings of the Somerset Archaeological and Natural History Society. Certainly there is much to be found therein that is illuminating, despite the learned dullness in which the bulk of the work is couched. But this is slow going at best. So for my own pleasure, and perhaps for the interest of some others, I have spent these past winter evenings setting down the story of my beloved hill country as well as I am able, and in the hope that a picture, or pictures, in time may so be presented, that they may join those many in space which already exist.

For what it is worth, here it is.

1968   H. L. B.

1. THE HILLS

AND THE FIRST FOOTSTEPS

Long ago, long ago—where does the story begin? Perhaps with the beginning of the world itself; perhaps with the red sands of some 300 million years ago, sinking to the bottom of a sullen sea, slowly turning to stone while strange life splashed in the waters above; perhaps with the ocean bed upflung by cataclysmic force into a mighty mountain range; perhaps with the mountains worn down by the weather of aeons to the stumps that have become the hills of the western land today, a wilderness of wild things and a birthplace of rivers.

We are human, though, and a tale told must be of men, and of things seen through the eyes of men.

IN THE BEGINNING

What feet then first trod upon these hills, and what was the scene that lay before them? Perhaps the first glimpse that we can catch of that far-off beginning of things is some time long ago about the end of the last Ice Age, when small bands of Palaeolithic hunters may have come pushing their way slowly up the river valleys in the wake of ever-moving game, gradually following their quarry up to the high ground. The period might possibly be some 20,000 years ago, and the climate still cold, though the snow and icy weather that had spilled down from the north for so many thousands of years had at last begun to

I

retreat, so that life in the region was tolerable for hardy human folk.

HUNTERS OF THE STONE AGE

These first hunter folk would have been of a tall strong race, physically not so very different from the average person of today, but their clothing was all of skins, and their tools and weapons were only of bone or flint, and they were ever on the move after the wild things upon which their whole life and living depended. Human culture had barely dawned, and mankind knew nothing of existence beyond the tracking and slaying of beasts, the fullness of food or the bitterness of starvation, the sun or rain by day, the warmth of a camp fire at night, and perhaps the security of a cave in the long winter months. The land about them, as they wandered westwards and towards the north, would have had much the same contours as today, but would have been covered mostly with a scrub of willow and birch, and the hills would rise before them prairie-like against the sunset. If a few of them ascended the narrowing valleys to the heights and stood upon the hill top that is Dunkery they would see before them a wide marshy plain where is now the Severn Sea, a huge swamp-like expanse threaded through with a broad river, and, beyond, far to the north, the white glitter of mountains still capped with snow and the ice of glaciers. All about them, on the hills and in the thickets and on the marshes below, the land would hold herds of game of many sorts. There would be deer and wild horse, wild ox, bison, elk, wild boar and reindeer perhaps, and beasts of prey too, such as wolf and bear and lynx. There might too be a few mammoths left, ponderous hairy monsters wandering still along the far edge of their frozen territory, and perhaps a last woolly rhinoceros wallowing in the plain of the Severn.

Also—because at that time the land of Britain was still joined to the continent of Europe, and Europe to Africa, and wild beasts were free to roam from the tropics to the Arctic—

there might be occasional lions and panthers venturing as far north as they dared, seeking like man the prey that was their livelihood. This south-western country of Britain probably had a very rich and varied fauna at that remote time, for it lay at a point where the extremes of the northern and southern climate met; the line of the Severn estuary seems to have marked a boundary that was the southernmost limit of the ice-sheet at its greatest extent, and the hills of Exmoor, though they must have been swept by bitter winds and snow, were never under glaciation, a fact that is obvious from their contours.

The hunter folk came and went. They left no mark upon the hills. Only now and then careless or forgetful fingers let fall a flint, an arrow-head or scraper, which after many centuries of time might be found again to give proof of their ancient passing. (A little while ago I held one of their scrapers in my hand—a small neatly chipped thing, fitting nicely between thumb and fingers, quite as good as, and perhaps better for its purpose than, the steel skinning-knife with which I recently flayed a calf-skin.) But the little wild horses remained, whose hides and meat had drawn the hunters to the hills—for horse-flesh was a favourite food of the ancient folk—and we see them still, even today, little changed by the passing of many centuries, and appearing just as they must have done to the eyes of the ancient hunters of so long ago.

NEOLITHIC FOLK

After a long while, many thousands of years, a further change began to come over the land. The climate slowly grew milder and wetter and great forests of oak and ash and beech grew up and covered all the country until only the high hills and the mountains rose above the tree line. The animals of the plains departed, and only those beasts who were suited, or could adapt themselves, to the wet forest conditions remained. At the same time something else was happening : gradually parts of the land were sinking, and the ever-hungry sea was making those inroads that were finally to sever Britain from the rest of the continent for ever. To the north of the Exmoor hills the Severn plain was slowly succumbing to the invasion of the ocean, though it would not be entirely engulfed for many long centuries, perhaps not until the beginning of historic times.

Along the tangled swampy river banks a few Mesolithic fisher folk may have lived out their lowly lives, spearing fish and gathering what other foodstuffs they might find, forgetful of the mighty hunting days of the past, and knowing only the pressing shadow of the forest. Otherwise there were none to break the heavy silence but the creatures of the woods and the birds of the tree tops.

In 3000 B.C.—or thereabouts—another sort of men began to venture westwards through the forests about the feet of the hills. They were folk small in stature, and dark, with long-shaped heads, and they seem originally to have come from the far-off shores of the Mediterranean. As they moved upwards and onwards, they drove with them flocks and herds, for they had at some time in their past history discovered that certain animals could be domesticated, and man was thus freed from complete dependence upon hunting. They had cattle and pigs and dogs, and an animal new to Britain—the sheep. They also had knowledge of simple weaving and pottery-making, and where they settled, in places sufficiently free from dense forest, they sowed little plots of corn for extra food. In fact they were Britain's first farmers.

Did they come up to the high hills? If so they also came and went without leaving any trace of their passing—unless indeed they left us the horned sheep as a legacy from their wanderings. It is likely enough, for our horned sheep of today, though considerably improved above the most primitive types, nevertheless represent one of the oldest sorts of British sheep. That they settled in the lower country about the moor, though, we we can be fairly certain, for so many of our people today have the dark hair and eyes and fineness of feature that were characteristic of the Neolithic folk, and which must be an inheritance from that distant forgotten past.

PEOPLE OF THE BRONZE AGE

Then, as time moved between 1800 and 1000 B.C., there came westwards to the hills, from over the sea, a new race of men, more dominant, more positive than the earlier shadowy folk, a people who have left the mark of their hands upon the moor for all ages, and their monuments for our eyes to see. Who were they? We cannot say for certain. All that we do know of them is that they were a part of that fierce surging movement of races that disturbed the whole world about the beginning of the second millenium B.C., and whose centre of radiation seems to have been the steppes of western Asia. These new folk reached our shores in many successive waves, like spent surf on a distant beach, and for them the archaeologists have invented many different names, such as Beaker Folk, Battle-Axe Folk, Urn People, Goidels and others, and their culture they have divided into periods of Early, Middle and Late Bronze Ages. In general it may be said they were all fragments of a group of races that we have come to call 'Indo-European' or 'Aryan-speaking'. The names of science, though, mean no more to us here than a confused noise or sound. All that we are sure of, or all that matters, is that at some time before 1000 B.C. a new race, some tribe of the new folk, came up to the hills with their flocks and herds, and dwelt on or about the high moor, and raised the round barrows on the lonely skylines and the mysterious standing stones on the long slopes.

It is with these folk that the history of Exmoor may be said to begin, so we should look well, or as well as we are able, at both them and the land as they found it, for it is on these two forces—man and the earth—and their constant interaction, each one moulding the other, that the whole structure of history rests.

One tries then to visualize the land as it was, as yet untouched by the hand of man, and as it must have appeared to these first colonizers. Thick oak forest, mixed with ash and beech, must have blanketed all the land about the hills, eastwards to the marshes of Athelney, southwards to the tors of Dartmoor, and westwards to the ocean until the salt sea winds cut back the growth to the very ground. From out of the green muffling forest would rise the heights of Exmoor, all their combes and goyals [1] choked with scrub of hazel and rowan and thorn, and their hurrying streams fringed with alder and sallow. High up the flanks of the hills the thinning bush of wind-stunted growth would struggle, feet in the heather, until it could go no farther, because upon the skyline ridges that same salt wind bit back all things but grass and heather. Here upon the plateau of the heights was open country and wide dry pasture. The climate on the whole seems to have been somewhat drier at this time than either before or since, and it is possible that the deep bog-peats had not yet formed, and that the high central ground was thus a drier and a firmer terrain than it is today. There were probably trees too along the fringe of the timber line that have since disappeared in the natural state—trees such as the lime and the 'Scots' pine. (Recent pollen analysis from certain parts of the moor seems to bear this out.) Beyond the hills, on the far north side, the sea carved its way inland to meet the Severn, but as yet there was much swamp land about the estuary, all of it overgrown with jungle forest of oak and dark primeval yew.

Game there was in plenty. In the forests there were many beasts, red deer and roe deer, the aurochs with its mighty horns, the elk, wild boar, wolves and possibly bears. Upon the more open heights herds of wild horses grazed. Lower down the valleys, where the rivers met the forest, there were beavers. In the sky above wheeled the eagle and hawks of many sorts, and birds now departed, such as the crane and the pelican.

The new folk, whether they came overland through the forest or by way of the coast, drifting down the big river in canoes and rafts, would see the hills rise against the westering

[1] Rocky clefts or small valleys.

sun like a promised land, high, dry and open, skylines clear of the choking forest, offering pasture for beasts and dwelling-space for man. So they came and took possession, and they and their race abode here for perhaps a thousand years.

When they reached the hills, though, it is unlikely that they settled in any way upon the upper heights—for even though drier, the hill tops must have been then as now very windswept, and often battered by ocean gales—but more likely had their dwelling-places, such as they were, on more sheltered ground near the tree line. Very probably they were a people largely nomadic in their habits, as was in keeping with their way of life, dwellers in tents and booths rather than in established settlements, who followed their flocks and herds up to the high pastures in the summer months, and returned with them to the more sheltered lower regions for the winter season. (This guess is borne out by the fact that there are very few remains of any sorts of prehistoric dwellings upon Exmoor, as against the hundreds of hill-top barrows that still exist.)

These people of the hills, these folk whose hands raised the barrows and the mysterious standing-stones—things silent yet so eloquent—whose feet trod out the ridgeways that our roads follow even now, what was their life and what can we know of them, they who have left us no written word or other voice? To what purpose did they set up their strange stones, and with what mystic ceremonies were their barrows and their circles hedged about? What were their gods, their loves and hates, and what was the world to them? Alas, we cannot know in full, nor very clearly at all even in part, but much we can guess, partly from other coeval sources, partly from the evidence of circumstance, and partly—this most of all perhaps—from the eye of imagination. We know that these folk were akin to all the other restless Aryan-speaking Indo-European races who were taking their place in the world about that time, that they were, more or less, contemporary with the Achaean and Trojan 'horse tamers' of the Homeric Bronze Age (*c.* 1200 B.C.), and that they were most probably of substantially the same race (though somewhat removed in time) as the heroes of the Irish tales and epics (surely 'Dunkery' is a name of the Gaelic or Goidelic tongue?) It seems not too wild a guess to suppose that their general culture and life, though of necessity of a standard far below that of their more polished and affluent kinsfolk, having neither the gold of Mycenae nor the harps of Tara, yet shared a background common to all others of like origin. With this in mind, let us try to see again these folk upon the hills.

HUNTERS AND PASTORALISTS

One can picture them as a people of great vigour, physically strong, dominant, adventurous and restless, in character fiercely individualistic, and by nature warriors, hunters and pastoralists. As to their appearance, the indications are that they were of sturdy build, predominantly round-headed, square-jawed, fair-haired and probably blue-eyed—totally different from, and in complete contrast to, the earlier Neolithic folk. (The remains of such a man were found many years ago near Broomstreet, Culbone, and his skull, even today, fleshless and over 3,000 years old, still conveys such a sense of force and vigour as to leave no doubt of the energy and determination of such a person in life.) These folk, by necessity of their hunting and herding ways of life, would be largely nomadic, moving from place to place with their herds according to the seasons. They would be grouped in tribes or communities under the rule of warrior chieftains, or petty kings, who would not infrequently engage in trivial wars or cattle raids against each other. Their wealth would be in their herds of cattle and flocks of sheep, and in their horses—for these folk were of the horse-taming peoples who somewhere in their steppe-land past had learned to bridle the head of the wild horse and tame him to their uses—though they also would sow patches of corn where the ground was suitable, or they were sufficiently settled for seed time and harvest. They hunted much, partly to supplement their food

A BRONZE-AGE ENCAMPMENT

supplies, partly to destroy predatory wild beasts and partly without doubt for sport. Their hunting-hounds, like their horses, were a source of great pride to them. They had knowledge of pottery and weaving, and delighted in such bright colours as they were able to find to dye their simple clothing. They also had knowledge of the working of metals, especially bronze, which new-found alloy gave name to the whole period and to its peoples.

Our people of the hills no doubt erected temporary dwellings of tent-like nature, simple edifices of varying size and shape, composed of sapling poles covered over with hides or coarse cloth, or thatched with heather or rush. With a camp fire at the

open end and rushes and pelts to lie upon, they would be com-
fortable enough except in the very depths of winter, when all
things had to struggle to live. The place of the chieftain would
be no different, except in its greater size, and that it might have
a palisade kraal-wise about it. Here in the light of the fire and
the stars, before the audience of the warriors, a bard might
chant his songs, tales of gods and men, of wars and raids, of
heroes and princesses, of hunting and harvest and sorcery, and
the fates that ruled all life. The firelight might shine on the
winking blades of the spears leaning against the roof poles, and
on the wheels of the wickerwork chariot that is the lordly pride
of the chief, and glitter on the small ornaments of gold under
the rapt bearded faces, while the cooking-pots hiss with the
sweet odorous steam of broiling meats, and all around, beyond
the reach of the light, is the darkness of the unknown night and
the spirit of the darker earth.

The speech of these folk was probably some early form of
Celtic, and a love of eloquence in them from the beginning.
Poetry is the oldest of the arts, for it alone needs no housing and
imposes no weight to carry, and needs only a mind to hold it
and a tongue to give it life. As to the mundane things of daily
life, the cattle of the hill folk would be the same long-horned
beasts of former times not far removed from the wild, and their
sheep no doubt the same horned sort as those of their Neolithic
predecessors. Their horses would be the little wild ponies of the
hills, caught and tamed with bridles of hide and twisted withies
and saddled with the skin of a wolf. Their hounds would be big
brutes, wolf-like and savage, equally able to pull down a deer or
tackle a boar. The corn that they grew—if in fact they did so
here on the high ground—would be some sort of barley or rye.
Whether or not they made hay for the winter we do not know.
Their tools in daily use were probably still of stone or antler, for
bronze was the metal of princes and was not to be afforded for
menial work.

All around them was the power of nature, savage, beautiful

and cruel. It governed their lives in all things, making the difference between plenty and starvation, life and death. So their gods were the personification of the elements. Chief in their pantheon was the sun, the giver of life, the male principal. Nearer to them was the spirit of the earth, the great mother who brought to birth all things. Then there was the moon, also a female principal, and the stars, and all the spirits of wind and rain and storm, and the running rivers. Even the springs and trees had their dryads and the caves and dark places their goblins. On all these, one or another, depended the success or failure of the harvests, the fertility of the herds and flocks, the health of the people. They had to be propitiated, these mighty ones, by sacrifices and with chants and ceremonies, and so there were priests and priestesses and sacred places. The seasons of the year, the turning-points so vital to a pastoral people, would be marked by religious ceremonies, followed by feasting and general merrymaking. The most important of these dates, or divisions of the year, were May Day, the beginning of summer, when the beasts went up to the high pastures, and the last day of October, the end of summer and beginning of winter, when they came down again. Equal with these in the cycle of life— though less important to the herdsman—were the summer and winter solstices, Midsummer, the longest day of the year, and that which we call Yule, the shortest. All these we remember even today, under various names, though their meanings have ceased to matter so much.

RIDGEWAYS

So they lived, these hill folk of the Bronze Age, in their round of the herdsman's year, their lives occupied with herding and hunting, punctuated with annual festivals, and enlivened doubtless by quarrels and fights, either amongst themselves or with such remnants of the little dark Neolithic folk as must have survived somewhere about. If their lives were circumscribed according to our standards, at least they were far from dull, and anyway birth, death, marriage and scandal are the same in every age and place. There were travelling merchants too in those far days, traders who slowly made their way from end to end of the land and even over the sea, bartering jet and amber, gold, bronze weapons, furs, perhaps bright dyed cloths, and, best of all, tales of far-off wonders and giant things unbelievable —even perhaps of the great new temple of Stonehenge. Slowly the ridgeways were being beaten out and the first highways evolving to link one end of the country to the other.

The legacy that our Bronze Age folk have left us falls roughly into five categories: ridgeways, barrows, circles, menhirs or standing-stones, and one great clapper bridge. The ridgeways that their feet beat out, seeking always the high dry ridges and the most direct ways from one side of their territory to another, answered so well the purpose that many of these ancient tracks carry to this day our modern roads busy with motor-cars and heavy lorries. The main road from Dulverton over Winsford Hill to Withypool is part of one ancient way, the rest of which continued by the line of what is now Ketteridge Lane, over Bradymoor, to join the main east–west route at Prayway Head. Another way went from the fords of the Barle at Dulverton up to Anstey Barrows and on into Devon (the line of the present 'Molland Moor Gate' road). Yet another went up from Dulverton by Hawkridge Ridge to Sandyway. From Sandyway a track ran along the western ramparts of the hills to Mole's Chamber, where it probably dropped inland to go on to Saddle Gate. A northerly route rose from Porlock Hill and ran along the crest of the coastal hills towards Countisbury (the present main Porlock–Lynmouth road). The principal highway though, that known in later times as Prayway, was the central track that rose to the Brendons at Elworthy, and followed the Brendon Hill ridge to Quarm or thereabouts, went on to Exford, then ran all along the watershed above the Exe, by Prayway Head, and from there on into Devon, probably by Duredon and the dry side of the Chains. In addition to these main ridgeways there were numerous subsidiary or connecting routes, such as one by way of Tarr Steps, or from Withypool to Sandyway by Green Barrow, or probably from Prayway Head by Brendon Two Gates to the sea. Strange how these ancient ways should have endured as highroads through the ages.

ROUND BARROWS, CIRCLES AND LONGSTONES

Of all the monuments left to us by these folk, it is the barrows that are most dominant, looking down to us as they do from every ridge and hill top, and drawing our eyes to them as with some strange compelling force. Mounds sunk deep in the heather and rush, what tales do you tell? What ashes lie in your depths, what spirits hover with the kestrels in the wild west wind? Chieftains, warriors, bards, forgotten and nameless heroes of a vanished age and race, theirs are the lonely hill tops and nights of stars and storm. For these are the burial mounds of the men of long ago, where once their ashes were laid to rest after the flames of the funeral pyre and the days of stormy life. With what rites they were interred we do not know, nor what were their hopes of future life, or whether feasting and games accompanied their departure to the realms of the great unknown, but here are the mounds raised over the urns, and there is no darkness about them, no fear or desolation of the soul, no dread. Tragedy perhaps, as companion to a violent life, grief and the lust for vengeance, but not hopelessness. It is the light of the sun that one feels, not the darkness of the earth, here by the broken-rimmed round barrows.

The barrows of Exmoor are legion. They crown every high place upon the moor, sometimes single and solitary, sometimes in groups, and all are of a simple round form. Most of them incline to a certain hollowness in the middle, though whether they were originally so, or have worn thus with the centuries of weathering, would be hard to say. They vary in size from the quite small to the imposingly large, and certainly all must have been much higher in their original state—consider the weathering-down of three thousand years, and the difference in height that this must have made.

The most imposing group of all is that of 'Five Barrows' upon Span Head, the second highest point of Exmoor and the dominant one of the long western rampart. There are in point of fact seven (or eight) barrows in this group, but the name 'Five Barrows' has become attached from the peculiar fact that only five can be seen upon the skyline from any one point of observation. (From far off, especially from the very easternmost heights of the moor, one can pick out the five barrows in a row like dots on the distant skyline.) The largest group is that of Chapman Barrows, high above the north-west corner of the moor. There are eleven, I believe, somewhat scattered about on the wide hill top, and the biggest one is unfortunately broken by a fence. Two or three together is a usual number. Wambarrows, upon the summit of Winsford Hill, consists of three in a row. There are three in the Longstone Barrow group and two together at Brightworthy Barrows. As to all the others, many are well-known landmarks—Black Barrow, Woodbarrow, Green Barrow, Setta Barrow and the like—whilst many more are nameless and half forgotten.

Some of the barrows have been excavated, but nothing of any consequence has been found. No golden horse-trappings as at Mold in Flintshire, no beaker of gold as from Rillaton in Cornwall. The hill folk were not affluent, or perhaps they were too worldly wise to sacrifice their treasures.

As to the stone circles, there are at least three on Exmoor. The largest, or so I should judge, is that upon the westward slope of Withypool Hill. It has some thirty or forty of its small upright stones still standing, though until recently they were hard to mark in the deep heather. The swaling of the heather across this patch a year or so ago has now revealed them more clearly. (Incidentally this ancient circle is not placed exactly as marked on the ordnance map; taking Withypool Hill Barrow as a starting-point, one has to look in a slightly more northerly direction than that given on the sheet.) A second circle is at the head of Colly Water just below the Hawkcombe Head–Lucott Cross road. This seems smaller, or at least has fewer stones standing, but like the former one has a western aspect. The third is above Chetsford Bridge. There may be others, partial and not yet recorded, about the lonelier parts of the moor, though I do not know of any. There seem to be fragments of stone rows in places, though in many cases it is hard to judge what is the handiwork of man and what the vagary of nature.

These little brethren of Avebury and Stonehenge were doubtless small sacred enclosures of some sort, serving as focal points for seasonal religious gatherings and ritual ceremonies; little temples of the sun perhaps, though only one of them has an easterly aspect. Few of the remaining stones are more than knee high, and many are less, though the weather of ages and the rubbing of beasts may have worn some of their size away.

Most mysterious of all are the standing-stones, the single lonely menhirs that thrust up from the sullen earth in various parts of the moor. (Or used to, perhaps one should say, for of those known to have existed all but a very few have now disappeared, wrenched out no doubt for handy gate-posts at the time of the late enclosures.) Of those surviving the finest and most impressive is the Longstone high upon Challacombe Common, set between Longstone Bog and Chapman Barrows, near the head of Swincombe. It is a strange thing, this tall thin slab of slaty stone, some nine feet high, wedged with a smaller stone at its base, and set to face southwards just below the ridge of the skyline. It has a peculiar form, and a strangely dominant presence, far from inanimate, almost giving you the impression that it in some way perceives you as you pass it by. What could have been its purpose? A memorial? A boundary mark? A sacred symbol? No one knows. One can only guess at its meaning, and at the dark fierce things bound up within its being.

There is, or was, another Longstone near Hawkridge. This and various others in medieval times served as markers for the

Forest bounds—as also did certain of the barrows. The Edgerly Stone still exists, incorporated into the roadside wall near the county boundary. The Sloley Stone, the Hore Stone and the Bill Hill Stone have all left their names, if not their presence, to parts of the moor. The Saddle Stone, a small, squat, curiously saddle-shaped stone, is set by Saddle Gate, on the way down to Shallowford. The 'Caractacus Stone' on Winsford Hill, probably the best known of all the Exmoor monoliths, is either of a much later date, or else had its inscription carved upon it a thousand years afterwards.

TARR STEPS

One great cyclopean bridge, the finest in the West Country, perhaps in all England, stands as example of Bronze Age clapper construction. This, Tarr Steps, marches across the River Barle at a point some three miles (as the crow flies) below Withypool, and must have been erected for the purpose of connecting the two high ridgeways of Winsford Hill and Hawkridge. Indeed such a work would surely have been constructed only on a route of great importance, and inclines one to think that a main highway in ancient times came down to the water here, one running perhaps diagonally from the Brendons over Winsford Hill and the Hawkridge moors into Devon. (Incidentally one hears in the Middle Ages of a 'great way' that runs somewhere up from Exford to the Wambarrows and thence 'between the two Ashways' down to the Barle.)

Tarr Steps (in olden times call 'Torr') is a fine sight, especially when the water is running high and racing under the stones with noise and foam, for here the river is wide and the valley deep and wooded. The bridge takes the water in some fifteen strides, each great clapper resting on buttressed piers of other stones, and the horseman's ford runs broad beside it, linking the ends of road that come to the river here. The mottled shadows of trees play on the huge blue stones, and the sound of the water fills one's ears; and one wonders at the mighty weight of the clappers, and tries to guess from what quarry they could have come and how they were hauled to the river bank. The answers we do not know, but here are the stones today, and the river runs fast beneath them still.

Some folk have declared that Tarr Steps may be no older than the pack-horse days of the Middle Ages, yet there can be no reasonable doubt that these cyclopean blocks are one with the longstones and the barrows. Certainly, Tarr Steps has been breached and down numerous times in its history, for the Barle is a stormy river—the last occasion was the great flood of 1952— but always local hands have sooner or later found time and tackle to raise the mighty stones again. Maybe it was rebuilt in the Middle Ages, but the clappers were ancient then, and lay as they fell on the river bed.

Incidentally the word 'torr' seems identical with the Dartmoor 'tor', both meaning stone or rock.

What fate ultimately befell our Bronze Age hunters and herdsmen we do not know. There are indications that some time after 1000 B.C. the general climate of the high ground began to get wetter again, approaching the rainfall and conditions that hold today. Mist and rain would wrap the hills, especially on the western side, the ground would become more waterlogged, the peat deeper, the bogs black and malignant. Perhaps the hill folk moved gradually down to lower ground, preferring the forest, in winter at least, to the rawness of the heights.

Perhaps, though, they did not go of their own free will, but were dispossessed by another people with mightier weapons. For about this time fresh invaders, armed with iron swords, had reached Britain and, like others before them, were pushing north and west in search of land and homes.

IRON AGE CELTS

About 500 B.C. a new race, or at least a fresh branch of an old one, began to cross to Britain from the continent. These were the Iron Age Celts, a people who had acquired the knowledge of the working of iron, and so were the masters of folk who only had weapons of bronze. Sooner or later they too came westwards to the hills, and took possession like the Bronze Age folk before them. Certainly whatever the state of the weather at that time, they did not find the climate displeasing, for they stayed upon the high moor to build numerous deep-ditched high-banked hill forts, which they would hardly have done if they had not occupied the land.

The Celts were a proud, restless, warlike people. In general, one may picture their life as being similar in most ways to that of their Bronze Age predecessors. Like them, they were hunters and herdsmen, tillers of the soil when conditions were favourable, and probably had little difference in the matters of custom and religion. Their use of iron and the knowledge of blacksmithing, however, would give them great advantages and lead ultimately to a somewhat higher standard of living.

The contemporary Celtic lake village of Glastonbury in eastern Somerset, though a far cry from the stormy heights of Exmoor, can give us some general idea of the daily life of the Iron Age folk, and what sort of stock they possessed.

These folk had horses and chariots, small shorthorn cattle (the 'Celtic Shorthorn', so called because it first appeared with the Iron Age Celts), sheep (uncertain whether horned or not), goats, pigs, dogs and fighting-cocks. The wild animals about them were red deer, roe deer, wild boar, wild cat, marten, otter and, most remarkable of all, beaver. (Wolves of course would be unlikely to haunt the meres, but would no doubt abound in the hill and forest country.) As to birds, as well as species common today, there were cranes, bitterns, divers, puffins and pelicans. The folk of the village grew barley, had tools and weapons of iron, ornaments of bronze, jet, amber and glass, and dwelt in huts of timber, and were skilful smiths, weavers and potters.

In the hill country, though, the pastoral folk probably still dwelt mostly in tents. The possession of iron axes, however, would enable them to fell timber more easily, and make clearings for settlements in the forest if they so desired.

HILL FORTS

It is the hill forts that are the dominant memorials of the Iron Age Celts on Exmoor. All about the moor one can find them, encircling the tops of steep hills with their crumbling earthen ramparts and rush-grown ditches, strange scars speaking of forgotten wars long ago. Countisbury, Berry above Hawkcombe, Staddon and Road Castle near Exford, Mounsey Castle and Brewers Castle above the Barle, Cow Castle higher up the river, Shoulsbarrow Castle, Stock and Roborough—these are some of them. The presence of these forts, or fortified camps, argues a warlike people, or at least a people well versed in war. These fortified enclosures most probably represent the kraals of petty chieftains, lords who were in a more or less constant state of war with one another, living in a society where cattle raiding was the natural order of things. (Into these enclosures cattle could be driven when some specially organized raid was anticipated.) Or the enemy might have been the older Bronze Age folk, and the hill forts the only means by which the new race could hope to keep their hold on the hill country.

The forts themselves vary a good deal in size, and also in form. Shoulsbarrow and Countisbury enclose quite a lot of ground, but Cow Castle and Brewers are very small. Shoulsbarrow and Road are roughly rectangular, while most of the others are round or irregular. With all of them the once-high banks are now worn and crumbling and the ditches almost filled in, just hollows rank with rushes. Once, though, the ditches were deep, and the earthen ramparts lofty and steep and possibly crowned with spiked palisades. One wonders what scenes of violence were enacted before and about these castles of hill and earth. In times when the more lethal engines of war had not been devised, and local warfare was rather on the level of a somewhat deadly brawl, these hill forts must have been very difficult to take. Imagine oneself, having exchanged mutual insults with the defenders of the fort, trying to run or scramble as fast as possible up the steep face of an Exmoor hill, in the teeth of missiles, and burdened with a cumbersome spear and shield, and then at the top blundering into a swampy ditch, scrambling again up a precipitous bank, to come at last, breathless and near beat, face to face with an enemy who had had no exertion other than that of waiting. The most obvious way of reducing such a fort would be by siege, hoping by starvation or, more explicitly, thirst—the weakness of the hill fort was lack of water—to overcome the resistance of the defenders. But a midnight sally by men who knew the terrain much better than you could make such tactics unpleasant. So things might go on for a few days, until a good time had been had by all, and then, if neither side saw any immediate chance of exterminating the other, a truce could be arranged.

THE FIRST FARMS

Gradually, however, the peoples of the land attained political cohesion of a sort. At some time during or before the last century B.C. the warring tribes of the west were welded into the Celtic kingdom of Dumnonia, which kingdom or confederacy was to endure into the eighth century in Devon, and to the tenth in Cornwall. It is probable that it was in this time of the western kingdom, when life was a little less stormy than it had been, that those first isolated Celtic farms, which we know to have existed here and there in the hill country, came into being. Celtic or 'Welsh' place-names are few in the country about Exmoor, but some do exist that seem to be of that ancient origin. Triscombe, Treborough, Langaller, Rhyll, and possibly Dunster, stand out from the great mass of subsequent Anglo-Saxon names that flood the ordnance map, and the Saxon prefix 'wal' is in itself a probable indication of earlier Celtic settlement. Walland, Wallover, Well—perhaps these and others of like name are the first made, the very oldest of all our farms, rooted deep in ancient Celtic yards and little odd-shaped fields. (Our West Country 'combe' is of course identical with the Welsh 'cwm', a Celtic word meaning a narrow valley, but it does not in itself imply a habitation.)

These Celtic farmsteads would most likely consist of just a group of huts—one of them a 'long house' to accommodate the master and his precious cattle and horses—surrounded by a palisade, and having about it some small enclosures for the growing of crops and the pounding of animals. Such settlements would not be numerous though, for the indications are that the population of the West Country in pre-Saxon times was not very large. The land for the most part would still be an un-claimed waste of moorland, scrub, and thick oak, ash and beech forest. Hill farming, from the very first, would be almost entirely pastoral. The wealth of the farmers, and of the com-munity, lay in cattle, and all the pattern of farming and the cycle of the year would revolve around the beasts. Amongst all ancient peoples cattle have held a position of almost magical significance, arising from their all-important role in the economy of agricultural life, and often the very gods were depicted or described as horned, and resembling bulls.

Incidentally the last waves of late Celtic or Belgic invasion do not seem to have reached the Exmoor country—they stopped somewhere short of these parts.

THE ROMANS

In the year A.D. 43 the Romans invaded Britain and began their systematic conquest of the country. The armies of the Emperor Claudius reached the south-west at the conclusion of their campaign against the Durotriges and other tribes, and made themselves the nominal masters of western land. The Dumnonii seem to have come to terms with the imperial power, or at least to have submitted without much of a struggle, for there are no records of any bloody battles in the west. Exeter was founded round about A.D. 50 to be the capital of the new province, and to serve as a port and a garrison town.

The wild hills of Exmoor, far to the north of the province, would have offered little attraction to the Romans in the ordinary way of things, had it not been for certain strategic considerations. It so happened that some time after the middle of the first century the fortunes of war brought the northern sea coast into the front line of affairs for a while. Though the Romans had subdued the south of Britain, across the waters of the Bristol Channel the Silures of South Wales still held out, and fought fiercely against the invaders. Now between the shores of what is now Glamorgan and the high cliffs of Exmoor is no great distance, and for so long as the Silures were active there was constant threat of possible attack by them across the water. Could they have crossed in sufficient numbers they might have established themselves in the hills, roused the native population, and attacked the Romans in the rear.

COASTAL SIGNAL STATIONS

It was to guard against just this possibility that the Romans established two small fortress signal stations upon the highest cliffs of the Exmoor coast: one at Martinhoe and the other upon Old Barrow Hill. Here from these lofty positions they could command the whole sweep of the Severn Sea, and signal to the war galleys below if anything suspicious should be discerned.

Recent excavations at Martinhoe have disclosed quite a lot about this signal station and its arrangement. The fort, which was situated on the high cliff top to the east of Heddons Mouth, was defended by strong double ramparts and ditches, plus a third outer line of defence, and the single entrance to each area was set on the opposite side to the other, so as to make a possible attack more difficult. Within the fort were two ranges of wooden buildings, which served as barracks for the men and quarters for the commanding officer. There were field ovens for cooking, and a furnace for the repair of arms. Signalling would have been carried out either by fires or by means of a heliograph, i.e. by the flashing of a polished shield or mirror in the sun. The garrison probably consisted of some eighty to a hundred men.

The fort was almost certainly built and maintained from the sea. It is possible to bring boats in to the beach at Heddons Mouth just below, and one can visualize the comings and goings of nineteen centuries ago quite easily—the big many-oared galleys standing a little way out, while smaller boats put off for the beach, and the men, once ashore, struggling up one of the cliff paths, laboriously hauling supplies and equipment for the fort above. The timber for the buildings they probably got locally, from the woods a little way inland, but everything else would have to come up from the beach.

One cannot suppose that the garrison enjoyed themselves very much in their lonely outpost of empire. Once off duty there was nothing to do and nowhere to go. Such local population as existed probably disliked them as much as native folk always do dislike an occupying power (though no doubt condescending to trade with them). Being southerners they probably hated the climate, especially when the thick white sea-fog shut them in, coiling about the fort like some malignant spirit-force. Nor could they get any wine locally either. Altogether their lot cannot have been an enviable one.

These two coastal forts are the only known Roman stations in the Exmoor country. There is no evidence to show that the Romans penetrated inland. Imperial coins have been found at various places on or around Exmoor, a few at Dulverton, Dunster and Selworthy, and some at Exe Head, but these do not necessarily imply Roman occupation—it is more likely that the coins came into the hill country by way of trade rather than otherwise.

THE KINGDOM OF DUMNONIA AND THE CELTIC PRINCES

After the fateful year A.D. 410, when the legions everywhere were withdrawn for the defence of the city of Rome, the old

Celtic kingdom of Dunmonia reasserted itself. Unlike the southern and eastern parts of Britain, the West Country beyond the Exe had never been Romanized, the Roman hold on the far west being no more than nominal. Hence a Celtic resurgence was natural and possible.

For a brief while, a twilight time, the Celtic princes reigned again, two hundred years or so before the oncoming hordes of Saxon sea pirates poured over the land and blotted out the ancient kingdom for ever. This was the age of myth and magic and hero tales, of jealous princes and warriors on horseback, of Christian missionaries and Celtic saints, of Arthurian legend and the shadow of the great king himself. It was an age too of Irish pirates and some settlers, for these wild folk soon began to bedevil the western coasts.

INSCRIBED STONES

Of this period Exmoor has two memorials: the Caractacus Stone on Winsford Hill, and one other inscribed stone near Lynton. The first, set a little to the north-east of Spire Cross, bears the inscription (very much worn) *Carataci Nepus*, which would indicate that it was erected by a kinsman of one Caratacus. The other, which is at Ilkerton, is inscribed with words that would seem to mean *Cavvdus son of Civilis*. The purpose of these standing-stones, like that of the earlier Bronze Age monoliths, is uncertain. Whether they were erected as memorials to the persons named, or raised by those persons in their own lifetime to commemorate some notable event, or perhaps to mark some boundary, we cannot now know. One thing, though, they do tell us, and that is that these Celtic nobles, though they may have reverted to a native Iron Age state of society, nevertheless retained their knowledge of and respect for the Latin speech they had learned from their Roman overlords.

One can imagine some prince riding a-hunting over the hills, clad in gaudy clothing, spear in hand, with wolf-skins under the saddle, his hounds running by his side, and behind him his henchmen on horseback. Or, armed for war against some quarrelsome rival, weighted down with heavy arms and barbaric ornament, part Roman, part Celtic. Times were turbulent without the *pax Romana*, and the hill forts probably occupied once again. When not actually hunting, fighting and cattle raiding, the princes can be thought of as sitting in their halls of timber and tenting, feasting and drinking, and indulging in their favourite pastimes of poetry, rhetoric and boasting.

SEA PIRATES

Alas for the Dumnonii, their days were numbered. The Anglo-Saxon sea pirates who had for so long harried the coasts of south-east Britain, were no longer content merely to raid. They had found the land good, and more to their liking than their own Germanic homeland, and were determined to settle and to possess the country for themselves. Very soon they were to reach the West Country.

2. FARMERS AND SETTLERS

Time moves on, the scene changes and we begin to look upon a different pattern of landscape. Still the forest and scrub climb up to the moor, and still the moor frowns down upon it with the scorn of solitude; but now the blanket of the forest is broken with clearings, the chequer of small fields shows amongst the trees, and here and there a curl of wood-smoke shows blue above a half-seen, half-guessed-at roof of thatch. Even upon the shoulders of the heather hills one may discern some tiny dwelling set as high as it dare climb upon the slope and crouched down tight against the wind. There are beasts in the tiny enclosures, and oxen at plough, and out on the hills there are small flocks watched by shepherds with their dogs. A race of farmers and settlers has come to the moor, and the hand of the Saxon is laid on the land.

THE COMING OF THE SAXONS

Of the West Saxon conquest of the lands south and west of the Somerset marshes we have little documentary evidence, and no very clear picture. After the initial landing of the chieftains Cerdic and Cynric somewhere about Southampton Water in 495, they seem to have pushed northwards to the downlands of the chalk, and there consolidated themselves, as it were, before turning their attention to the West Country. In 652 and 658 respectively, Cenwealh the Saxon fought two battles somewhere in the west against the 'West Welsh', defeating the latter on both occasions and opening the way into Somerset and Devon. In 682 it is recorded that Centwine defeated the 'Welsh' in another battle and 'drove the Britons in flight as far as the sea'. The place of the battle is not specified, and the flight of the unfortunate Britons is variously said to have been from mid Somerset to the Bristol Channel or from mid Devon to the Atlantic coast. In 695 King Ine of Wessex attacked and defeated Geraint, King of Dumnonia, somewhere in the west, and after this we hear no more of battles.

It would seem probable that the whole of the West Country as far as the Tamar was in Saxon hands by about 720. Henceforth the land would begin to settle down to the slow process of becoming an English countryside dotted with farms and hamlets and with a final pattern of fields carved from wood and marsh.

The surge of colonization would come later to the hill country than to the richer and more accessible lands such as mid Devon or the vale of Taunton. For many years the heights of Exmoor would rise above the slowly advancing tide of Saxon settlement, looking down inscrutably to where trees were being felled and sods turned upon the far lowland. Indeed it is more than likely that the harsh and remote moorland with its deep combes, far-seeing heights and narrow approaches formed, as mountain country so often does, a centre of resistance for those who still struggled against the hated invader. Here may have come the last draggled remnants of defeated armies, dispossessed and bitter chieftains, a fugitive prince perhaps, a few terrified women and children, all of whom were determined to struggle for their native independence for as long as they might. There would be a watch again on the outer earthworks of the high places, rendezvous in the few existing farms under the rims of the hills, and perhaps sallies and raids on any unwary Saxon settlers who came too close. This guess into a troubled past is not an idle one, for in 710 we

hear of King Ine building a fortress at what is now Taunton—
and against whom would he raise it but the troublesome folk
of the western hills? The whole of Devon itself was by now in
Saxon hands, and Celtic Cornwall far away.

SETTLERS IN THE HILLS

Resistance, or at least resistance in so relatively small an area,
cannot go on for ever, and Saxon prevailed about the hills, and
Celt gave way, disheartened and weary no doubt without an
Arthur to harden his hopes, and so at last the settlers from over
the sea took possession of the high hills and all that lay therein
and around. Some time about the end of the eighth century, or
at latest during the ninth, Exmoor and the hill country passed
with the rest of the land into the keeping of Wessex.

The Saxon settlement in the hills was from the first one of
small individual farms, of individual family effort, with each
little farmstead a unit of life in a wilderness of still wild countryside. The nucleated village with its system of communal farming, such as made up the pattern of most of the Midland
country, had no place here in the hills. A few villages below the
line of the moor, where the terrain was suitable to such, might
follow the Midland system of open-field farming—Braunton
was one, and South Molton probably another—but as one
approached the higher ground there would be only the isolated
farmsteads or at most a few hamlets of just two farms set
together. Three dwellings or more would probably be regarded
as urban! This hill-country pattern of individuality and isola-
tion was imposed chiefly by the nature of the country, which by
its climate and terrain enforced a mainly pastoral or grazier
economy rather than a truly agricultural one, but also perhaps
there was something in the nature of these sturdy pioneers—
for such they truly were—that urged them to go out into the
wilderness and raise their own roof-trees and fight their own
battles with nature. Perhaps they preferred 'a place of their
own', despite all the hardships and dangers, to the safer but less

SETTLERS BUILDING A FIRST FARMSTEAD

self-reliant community life. Hill country has a way of breeding
individualists. Be it as it may, this was the pattern of settlement
that was followed from the Saxon conquest to the thirteenth
century, by which time almost every place-name that we know
today was set upon the countryside.

Look at the sheets of the ordnance map that cover the
Exmoor districts. The commonest termination to the many
hundreds of farms all about the moor is 'cott' or 'cote', a
holding or little farmstead, and after that there are many
'worthys', 'combes', 'leighs', 'leys', 'fords', 'hills', 'slades'
and 'bartons'—old English words all, with a history running
back seven hundred or a thousand years and more.

What of the dispossessed, the Celts? Perhaps their plight was not so bad as it might seem. Possibly most of those who survived ultimately made their peace with the Wessex overlords and continued to live in the land until gradually they or their children were absorbed into the new order. Certainly they were not by any means exterminated, for a good proportion of the moor folk today show in their physiognomy undoubted strains of Celtic or pre-Celtic blood. If one looks again at the map one may notice a number of places bearing the prefix 'wal', 'wall' or 'well', which may quite well be derived from 'wealh', a Saxon word meaning 'foreigner'. The Saxons called all the Celts 'Weala' or 'Welsh' and their still-held land 'Wales', so it is not at all unlikely that these 'walls' and 'wells' actually meant 'the farm of the Welshman'.

FARMSTEADS AND STOCK

It must have been very much like the backwoods settlement of Canada—the first farmsteads must have been very small, like all pioneer settlements in a new land. A single roof-tree for a start, with hearth and house-place at one end, and standings for the precious beasts at the other. (Even today one may observe in almost every hill farmyard that the cow shippon joins immediately to the dwelling-house, with the main doors of both opening together on to the same stretch of cobbles—a tradition of building that is a survival from the days when both lay under one roof and formed a single dwelling.) Other minor buildings might then accumulate as needed, and they would automatically form a group around a central yard, all facing inwards, presenting blank walls to the outer world. This was the natural arrangement, compact for work and against the winter weather, and affording a good possibility of defence against possible raids by bands of outlaws or predatory neighbours.

The materials of which the homesteads were built would be those that lay nearest to hand. The Saxons were by natural tradition builders in wood, and in the lower forested regions their new dwellings would have been of timber and perhaps 'cob', but here on the hills where the thick woods were of scrub type but the surface stone was abundant, the buildings would no doubt from the first have been of stone. The thin bluish slate would have been gathered from the hillsides and set and laid in the rag-pattern that has not changed its form in all the centuries. Timber for the roofs would be provided by good ash poles, and the roofing finished off with a thatch that might be at first of rush, and then of rye straw.

As to the site, the first thing settlers would look for would be a south-facing slope where their holding would catch the sun, especially the precious sun of winter, and where the rise to the north or east would give them some shelter from the coldest winds. Also they would look for a spring of fresh water not too far away that might, without too much difficulty, be guttered down to the proposed site. Water is the first essential of life, especially with livestock farming, but here in the hills there is no lack of it, and many of the little farms could be set right down beside a merry stream. (One would have to remember, though, not to set one's yard too low, else one might be flooded out when the stream rose in spate.) Land that offered a fair depth of soil for the small but necessary bits of cultivation for bread corn would be hoped for too, but, as all too often in the hills, one would have to take what nature provided and not grumble too much about it. Once a farm site was established and settled it was seldom changed and rarely abandoned. Many, many times over the hill farms must have been rebuilt or enlarged over the centuries, but few of them will have altered the space of their yards, worn now to bedrock, and at their roots are the stones of their first making.

Having set up his roof and cleared and burnt the scrub from the immediate land, the farmer-settler would next set about making his first enclosures. This he would do by the simplest of expedients, that of throwing up steep earthen banks of sufficient height to be a check to livestock. Where the earthen banks might seem to need strengthening, he would perhaps face them with thin stones set upright—the immemorial 'dyking' of the moor. These first little fields would be of only a few acres apiece, just as much ground as a man might 'break' in a season, and their shape irregular as might happen to suit some small local need. Having established himself, so to speak, he would then very likely take in a larger area of moorland—that is if he were in a high heather region—which would serve him as an 'outfield', a useful big enclosure into which he could drive stock in the winter, and which he could leave rough or cultivate piecemeal as he so pleased. This 'infield and outfield' system, which seems to have been a basis of early hill farming, may have been borrowed from the Celts, and in practice was much the same thing as our present-day complement of 'inground and allotment'.

From the first these farmsteads would have been of varying size. The holding of a thegn or man of substance would naturally develop quickly into a farm of the courtyard type with many odd buildings for the housing of stock, stores and family retainers, and have large outfields attached to it. (It was such settlements as these that formed the nuclei of the later-day manors.) At the other extreme, the holding of a little man would remain very small, possibly just a single roof-tree, and a few acres of land enclosed in tiny fields.

The beasts of the farm were oxen, sheep and pigs, and perhaps ponies; and sometimes goats. The most important of these were the oxen, for they drew the heavy plough and also the rough sleds upon which the heavier and more cumbersome loads were moved, and later in life they provided beef and tough hides for leather. Cows perhaps gave a little milk, though cattle were not generally thought of as dairy beasts at that early time. The ponies too would have been highly valued, for riding and as pack-horses. The sheep gave wool and mutton and, like the goats, milk and cheese. Pigs could forage in the woods, and wax into pork on the pannage of acorns.

Whether the Saxon settlers brought stock of their own as they moved up to the hills, or whether they simply possessed themselves of such as they already found in the region, is hard to say. Certainly the mealy-nosed ponies and the horned sheep were the gift of the moor, and the red long-horned cattle would almost certainly have been here too, browsing perhaps in the combes in feral herds, awaiting the slow process of domestication that would in time produce the famous Red Devons that we know so well today. It may be noted in passing that as late as the sixteenth century we hear of herds of cattle in remote parts of Cornwall being left to wander and multiply in a practically wild state, and of their owners periodically hunting them down for slaughter as though they were beasts of chase rather than domestic animals. From this one may deduce that some tradition of red cattle being regarded as wild creatures must have lingered on in the wilder parts of the West Country, resounding like an echo from a distant and primitive past into a world where such things had all but disappeared.

DAILY LIFE

As well as his stock, the early farmer had such grain as he could grow for his own use, probably rye, perhaps a little wheat. The wild land around gave him ample fuel in the form of brushwood and peat. It also might give him game if he had the hunter's skill to take it, for there were deer in the woods, and perhaps wild boar, hares in the heather, fish in the river, and wildfowl of various sorts. If he could compete with the fox, the otter, the wild cat and the wolf, he might eat as well as they off the increase of the wild.

It was very much subsistence farming, to be sure. When the seasons were good the farm family had rude plenty and might forget past and future hardships for a while. When times were bad, the winter long, the spring delayed, the harvest time wet, then the spectre of starvation stalked about the farmstead, and both beasts and men might succumb to the sickness and death that followed its footsteps.

If, when things went well, there was surplus of produce above the home needs, then this might be taken down by the lonely tracks to some small township community beyond the foot of the moor which had become sufficiently stabilized to have a periodic market or fair—Barnstaple to the west was the chief trading centre for all north Devon and west Somerset, and was a borough as early as the reign of King Æthelstan—and there they would sell or barter the produce of the hill country for such things of artisan manufacture that they could not make for themselves.

Meanwhile, as the settlers struggled for establishment and as much security as they might have in so insecure a world, a new influence was at work around and amongst them. From the middle of the seventh century onward Christian missionaries, mystical Celts from Wales, or pious priests from Rome, had been busy among the West Saxons, striving to convert them from the worship of the dark northern gods to the brighter faith of the Church of Christ. Steadily the missionaries prevailed, and the kings of Wessex themselves embraced the new faith, and their people after them. So now here and there about the tangled land around the moor a tiny church might appear, itself little different from any farm building, and beside it a cell for some dedicated priest. Here were hope and faith for the people of the hills, comfort in distress, and strength against the dark and potent spirits that still lurked in the night woods and in the corners of men's minds.

So life would go on, a farmer's round of seasons, largely uneventful except for those occasional but inevitable happenings which enliven the existence of folk in all states of being— marriage, births, deaths, quarrels, the sudden murder, thefts, and as much scandal as could be hatched up. Now and again the hounds of some prince or noble might come hunting up the valleys, pursuing the deer up to the wind-swept heights, and calling the farm folk from their work with the deep baying of their voices. Perhaps on rare occasions folk might even see the king himself, which would be something to talk about indeed. Tradition credits the later Saxon kings with having a small palace or hunting-box at Porlock, to which they came in due season for the hunting of the big stags, and if this were so then the people on the eastern side of the moor might well be treated to exciting glimpses of royal splendour from time to time.

DANISH RAIDS

Along the coast, though, things were not always so uneventful. By 843 a fresh pirate-people, the Danes, had embarked upon their invasion of eastern England, and their longships were soon to round the Land's End and come prowling up the Bristol Channel. Though there was little wealth to tempt them in the stern coast of hill and cliff that marked the northern edge of Exmoor, the sight of a pirate galley cruising in the Severn Sea must have caused trepidation in the hearts of those who watched its passing. In 878 the threat became more than a passing fear, and the West Country trembled for a moment on the brink of a fresh Nordic invasion, for in that year the Danes massed together under the chieftain Hubba, and landed in force somewhere on the north Devon coast in what was probably meant to be the spearhead of a new conquest. The army of the men of Devon met and defeated them with great slaughter, so that they never came again in force. The place of battle is usually ascribed to Northam, beyond the estuary of the Torridge, where one particular piece of ground is known as 'Bloody Corner' from an ancient tradition of a massacre long ago, but there are also claims for Countisbury above Lynmouth as the site. Certainly the old camp on the hill top could have been, and probably was, refortified against the possible threat of invasion, but the place—the mouth of the Lyn—does not lend itself to a large-scale landing. The valleys are too narrow, the hills too hostile, and there is not the beaching for the galleys. Northam is the more natural choice.

In 918 Porlock was raided by a passing band of pirates known as the Lidwiccas, but they were beaten off by the Somerset folk, and forced to retire to Flat Holm, where they were ultimately starved out. After this, apart from the raiding of Watchet in 988, the coast of these parts seems to have been left more or less in peace.

The bitter battles that were being fought between Saxon and Dane in middle and eastern England, the courage of King Alfred, the weakness of Ethelred and the final triumph of Canute the Dane, seem not to have troubled the hill folk much. There is not a single Norse or Danish place-name anywhere about Exmoor to suggest that any Viking settler ever came so far west or was ever given land in the district. Anyway, in race and custom the Viking folk were closely akin to the Anglo-Saxons, and the nominal change of overlordship would mean little in terms of daily life.

It may have been, though, at this time of the Anglo-Danish kings, that the wastes of high Exmoor were first claimed as Royal Forest by the Crown. King Canute, like most men of his kind, was a mighty hunter, and would without doubt have been glad to claim any land with an abundance of deer as a private hunting-ground for himself.

THE MANORIAL PATTERN

At about this time too we find the countryside settled into that manorial pattern which was to remain the universal unit system and grouping of rural life throughout the Middle Ages and beyond, until it was superseded by the concept of the parish. How the English manor came into being is uncertain— whether it had always been so, the manor farm marking the original settlement of some thegn, and its dependent farm steads and lands deriving from the colonizing of his retainers; or whether, conversely, various unrelated holdings had, by the necessity of some sort of administration and acknowledgment of law, grouped themselves together under the protection of a thegn, is something that can only be guessed at. Be it as it may, the eve of the Norman Conquest finds all England grouped or divided—whichever way one chooses to look at it—into manors or country estates, each of which is the unit of life, law and taxation for the folk of the countryside.

For a while all seems to have gone quietly and without event in west Somerset, then in 1052 there was again violence and fighting in Porlock. It seems that Harold, son of Godwin, held the manor of Dulverton, while at the same time Algar, son of Leofric of Mercia, held that of Porlock. The house of Godwin and the house of Leofric were arch-enemies, and Harold, on being outlawed by the prevailing power, determined on revenge at the nearest point. He gathered together an army or pirate gang of sorts in Ireland, set sail for the Bristol Channel and fell upon Porlock, probably landing in the dark. The Porlock men, though taken by surprise, put up a hard fight, but were beaten back by the raiders and many slain. Then Harold 'took of cattle, and of men, and of property, as it suited him', and departed with the ill-gotten gains.

THE NORMAN CONQUEST AND THE DOMESDAY BOOK

Fourteen years later the impact of the Norman Conquest shook all England. The same Harold died a hero's death upon the hill at Senlac, and the whole country passed into the hands of William the Conqueror and his Franco-Norman barons. With that one battle the fate of England, and of its every farm and village, was settled. For this invasion was no mere raiding expedition, but systematic conquest. The possessions of every man who had opposed the new order were forfeit, and almost every acre of land was taken to be given in reward to those greedy foreign adventurers who had thrown in their lot with William, and who had thereby made his victory possible.

Of those grim years that followed upon the Conquest, when

the new lords rode down to the West Country to take possession of their newly acquired manors, and the erstwhile Saxon occupiers thereof were either reduced to servitude or turned away to go God knows where, local history tells us nothing. Then in 1084–5 comes that monumental stock-taking—the Domesday Survey and Geld Inquest, and in 1086 its published result, the great Domesday Book.

William, having a methodical mind and being desirous of knowing exactly what he had 'of land and of cattle and what rights he ought to have yearly from each shire', sent commissioners into every part of the country to inquire into the business and management of each and every manor, and to make detailed reports of the lands, stock and population therein. For William this was a measure for practical taxation, but for us the careful survey is an invaluable record of the folk and farms and farming of nearly nine hundred years ago. It brings the past very near to us too. Through phrasing and black-lettering of nine centuries we can hear the rattle of Norman horseshoes on the cobbles of many a West Country farmyard, and see the bureaucrats get down from their horses and enter into conversation with the lord's bailiff, and see him in turn call for the ploughman, the shepherd or the swineherd. . . . Were the commissioners local men of the shire, or did they come all the way from the capital? And did they believe all that they were told, or did they ride round the estates and see for themselves? How one would like to know.

For the West Country we have two Domesday editions, the Exon (or Exeter) codex and Exchequer book. The first gives far more detail as to stock, etc., and one has the feeling that this was the first made and original document, and that its contents were later copied into the latter in abbreviated form, leaving out whatever was deemed of no immediate importance.

The Domesday Book is very easy to read—the old Latin is curt and precise—but often very difficult to interpret in terms of everyday meaning. The old land-and-tax assessments seem just about as complicated as our modern system of rates-at-so-much-in-the-pound-on-assessment-of-value or schedule this-or-that. However, that does not concern us much. What does concern us is that here we have first-hand records of names and places and people and things, and through these can get a fair picture of the countryside of those days.

DOMESDAY MANORS OF THE HILL COUNTRY

The Domesday manors of the Exmoor country, those small estates that clung to the flanks of the wild hills, numbered some fifty-odd (*see* Appendix A). How the commissioners' tongues must have struggled with the raw and unfamiliar Saxon-English names, and how the clerks too must have racked their brains to get these names into something respectably Latinized!

The first thing that each of the entries gives is the name of the contemporary holder, followed by that of the last pre-Conquest owner. 'Drogo holds this . . . Alwin held it. . . .' It is a pitiful tale. Entry after entry gives the name of a new Norman lord superseding an older Saxon one. In one instance only, one solitary instance—that of Hawkwell—do we find a Saxon thegn still holding his manor. 'Ulf holds Hauechewelle. . . . He also held it . . .' Why was he allowed to continue in possession of his land, one wonders? Was he a 'collaborator'? And what happened to all the other erstwhile owners, the Ælmers and Edrics, the Alrics and the Alwins? Were they slain resisting the hated invader? Or merely driven out to become outlaws, or reduced to near bondage? And what of their wives and children? The harsh record of the Domesday is not concerned with such things. In the case of one minor manor, Bagley, given to Roger de Corcelle, there is mention that one Caflo holds this from Roger, followed by the terse statement 'he held it'. Evidently here Caflo the Saxon was allowed to remain as steward or under-tenant.

Possibly the thing that stands out most harshly from the Domesday Book is the wholesale collection of land into the hands of the great barons, so marking and making possible the beginning of the feudal system. Where in former times the manors were mostly held by the individual thegns whose homes they were, they are now but part and parcel of the vast holdings of various nobles. In many cases the Church and churchmen are amongst the greatest of the new landlords. Here in the West Country the Bishop of Coutances is one of the greatest land-owners—he holds amongst his many manors those of Culbone, Wilmersham, Molland, Gratton, Wallover, etc. Other big landowners in Devon and Somerset are William de Moine (or Mohun), lord of Dunster, Roger de Corcelle and the Comte de Moretain. Those lands that had belonged to the Old English royal house, or to the house of Godwin, passed into the hands of King William himself, and so we find Winsford, Dulverton, Molland and North Molton as royal manors held directly by the king and administered by a steward.

The manors of the Exmoor hill country vary considerably in size, ranging from the very small ones that were themselves but solitary farmsteads, like Lank Combe with its one ploughland and one villein, to the very large that were the nucleus of many homesteads, such as North Molton, with its hundred plough-lands and hundred-odd householders. Mostly though, they ranged from the small to the medium sized, with from about five to twenty households.

THE LANDS OF THE MANORS

The lands of each manor are given in detail, classed according to usage or potential. First comes the ploughland, the most important class of soil, and here begin the complications which can only be sorted out by a good deal of guesswork. One typical hill-country manor, Brendon, may be taken as an example from which to look at the Domesday system and classification as a whole:

'Radulf [de Felgheres] has a manor called Brandona which Alward Tochesone held on the day on which King

Edward was alive and dead, and it rendered geld for one hide. This can be ploughed by eight ploughs. Of it Radulf has in demesne half a hide and two ploughs, and the villeins have half a hide and six ploughs. There Radulf has seven villeins and six bordars and five serfs, and one pack-horse and a hundred and four unbroken horses, and twenty-five head of cattle, and eight swine, and a hundred sheep and thirty goats, and thirty acres of wood, and two leagues of pasture, and it is worth by the year a hundred shillings, and it was worth thirty shillings when he received it.'

Now what can be made of this? First of all, the estate is assessed for tax or geld on one hide of its land, and against this the geld was payable. The hide was an old English measure of land, which probably originated as that average amount of ground which an eight-ox team could plough in an average season, and this in the midland or lowland countries became standardized at 120 acres, though it might be considerably less in other parts. A quarter of a hide was a virgate, and an eighth a bovate, a 'one-ox land'.

The estate itself consists of the demesne, which is the home farm, plus the outlying holdings of the peasant farmers. Here is a complication for, when stock or other appurtenances are mentioned, one cannot be sure—unless they are specifically stated to be 'in demesne'—whether such are the particular belongings of the home farm or are the collective property of the estate as a whole. In most cases, though, one would suppose the former.

The ploughland, the carucate, is the measure of arable land, and to all intents and purposes is identical with the hide, being one and the same thing in both origin and extent. The ploughland of the hill country, however, is most certainly not one of 120 acres. It is a fair guess that it is something less than half—perhaps about forty acres. Exmoor, with its high altitude and wet climate, is traditionally a country of spring ploughing and spring-sown corn, and it is reasonable to suppose that its medieval ploughland was such as could be ploughed in that short season. (In the drier eastern regions ploughing would start in the early autumn and continue all through the winter—hence the large measure of 120 acres for the eastern ploughland.) If, then, one accepts the carucate as round about forty acres, the ploughlands of Brendon would total something over three hundred acres. But that a hill-country manor, even a prosperous one, should have so much arable in any one year is hard to believe. What seems most likely, in this and all other cases, is that it is the total area of land *capable* of being ploughed that is entered, regardless of the amount which might in fact be tilled in any one season—in short, the entire land of the estate less the steep cleeves.[1] This is borne out by the fact that on most manors the ploughs maintained do not by any means equal the ploughlands. (Wilmersham has land to five ploughs, but only two ploughs in use, while Winsford has sixty ploughlands, but possesses only fifteen ploughs.) Yet here at Brendon they do—it is one of the rare instances where this is so—and so perhaps this estate was indeed farmed to full capacity. Maybe Radulf went in for high-farming. It is significant that the value per annum of the estate increased by more than 300 per cent since he had it.

The plough itself, *carruca*, was the heavy wooden Saxon plough, complete with its team of eight oxen: 'Half a plough', which is occasionally mentioned, would be a team of four oxen.

As to the relative size and extent of the hill-country estates, small manors such as Bagley, Downscombe, Lank Combe, Wallover and parts of Exford are credited with but one ploughland. Most of the others with from two to ten ploughlands; Dulverton with eleven, Lynton twelve and Cutcombe fifteen. At the top of the table, as one might say, comes Molland with forty ploughlands, Winsford with sixty and North Molton with one hundred.

<hr>

[1] Hillsides.

Other classes of land are pasture, meadow and woodland. Brendon had two leagues of pasture (a Domesday league was probably about $1\frac{1}{2}$ miles), and other places had varying amounts, ranging from a few acres to several leagues. This pasture would be rough grazing, and was probably represented by outfield or an area of enclosed moorland. Meadow was a better sort of grassland such as one might cut hay off, and most places had a few acres of it. Probably it here consisted of bits of water-meadow along the stream-banks of some of the wider combes. Woodland, important as a source of fuel and building material, ranges from a few acres to several leagues. Brendon has thirty acres. It is to be assumed that only such woodland as could provide timber-trees is mentioned, no note being generally taken of the scrub that must have choked most of the valleys. In one or two places coppice (*nemusculi*) is specified—as at North Molton, where there is a league of such—and in one instance there is mention of 'dwarf woodland' (*silvae minutae*) which can only mean scrub. This latter is in Almsworthy, above Exford, and the area of such is given as thirty acres.

With regard to all these sorts and areas of manorial land, it is to be remembered that all such lands are given collectively—the manor itself was the unit of taxation, and that was all that concerned the Norman bureaucrats—and except where something is specifically stated as being in demesne, it is not possible to say precisely what of this ground went with the manor farm, what belonged to the outlying peasant farms or what was held in common.

Of the vast stretches of open moorland that lay beyond or lapped all around these Domesday manors, there is no mention at all. They were just 'waste', untaxable wilderness, and therefore merely ignored by the powers that be.

PEOPLE

Next we come to the people, the population. Three classes of folk are given: villeins, bordars and serfs. The villeins were the most numerous class, they were the people of the 'ville', or community, the peasant farmers, the tillers of the soil. They may once have been free men, but by the time of the Conquest and for a long while afterwards they were bound to the manor, and in return for the right to have land and a home of their own they had to render services to the lord of the manor, working on the demesne land a certain number of days in the year, and probably rendering other dues as well. The bordars, whose numbers were on the average considerably less than those of the villeins, were probably small-holders, peasant farmers like the former, but of lesser means and substance. At the bottom of the scale come the serfs, who were bondmen, no better than slaves, whose lives were at the lord's bidding. On the whole they were fewer in number than either of the other sorts of folk. In addition to these classes of person one sometimes comes across an individual who seems to have been of sufficient importance in his calling to rate special mention. Such was the professional swineherd—at Countisbury there was 'one swineherd who renders ten swine yearly'.

The population of the manors varied. At Brendon we find seven villeins, six bordars and five serfs. But at the lonely little moorland manor of Lank Combe there is but one solitary villein, all on his own, presumably looking after the place as bailiff for his lord. At the other extreme, there are at North Molton forty-four villeins, fifty bordars, eleven serfs, fifteen swineherds and four farriers.

As each of these persons argues a family—one presumes that only the man, the householder or able-bodied worker is given— and a wife and numerous children argue a home, one can guess at the number of little farmsteads within each manor. Though the serfs probably huddled in hovels near the manor farm, and craftsmen on the larger manors lived near the centre of things and made up the beginnings of a village, one may assume that the villeins and bordars had each a little holding somewhere amongst the folds of the hills and combes. They would come together at certain times to give the customary land-service to the lord of the manor, and they no doubt loaned their plough teams to one another just as a modern farmer lends his hay-baler to a neighbour, but for the most part they would live their own separate lives, for one cannot visualize any communal pattern of farming in the hill country even in early times.

FARMSTOCK

After the list of folk comes the stock. This consists of cattle, sheep, goats and pigs, and in some instances horses. Cattle were of great importance as draught oxen for the heavy wooden ploughs, and one may assume that those beasts (*animalia*) mentioned formed the breeding-stock and the replacements for the plough teams. At Brendon there were twenty-five beasts. On some of the smaller estates there are none, or at least none mentioned. On the average sized manors there might be from two to thirty beasts, and Lynton had fifty-eight head. At Radworthy (near Challacombe) two plough oxen (*boves in carrucam*) are specified, which is unusual.

Sheep, representing wool, mutton and possibly dairy products, existed in flocks of varying sizes. Strangely enough there is no mention of sheep at Brendon, but at Countisbury nearby there were '300 sheep less thirteen'. There are a few other places where no sheep are mentioned, but most of the estates had flocks of sorts, varying from the mere twelve at Rowley to the 287 at Countisbury, which is the largest number mentioned. These hill-country sheep were almost certainly the native horned sheep of Exmoor.

Goats, important for their milk and the cheese that was made therefrom, were kept in small flocks or herds. There were thirty at Brendon, just a few (eight) at Badgeworthy and as many as seventy-five at Lynton and Ilkerton. Presumably they were almost all she-goats, but of what type we do not know. Possibly they were similar to the present semi-wild goats of the Valley of Rocks—who knows, perhaps these very creatures are the feral descendants of the ancient peasant flocks of the district?

As to pigs, those creatures which satisfied our ancestors' love for pork, bacon and lard, they too were kept in herds. There were only eight at Brendon, it is true, and no more than three at Badgeworthy but, as we have seen, there were on certain manors men who were specifically swineherds, which argues the presence somewhere in the wilds of large roving herds of pigs. No doubt they foraged in the scrub-oak woods and waxed fat on the pannage of acorns, and very likely they were not far removed from the wild boar in either pedigree or habits.

EQUAS INDOMITAS

Lastly we come to the horses. By far the most interesting entries are those which specify wild or unbroken horses—*equas silvestres* and *equas indomitas*. Here without a doubt is the first historical reference to the little wild horses of Exmoor, ancestors of our present-day ponies. They occur in greatest numbers just where one would expect to find them, in the remote isolated northern parts of the moor. At Brendon there were 104 *equas indomitas*, and on the joint manor of Lynton and Ilkerton there were 72 *equas silvestres*. At Cutcombe on the south-east side there were 39 *equas silvestres*, and also seven at Luccombe and five at Horner, and two at Quarm. (What distinction, if any, might be made between the 'unbroken' and 'woodland' horses is not apparent. Both terms may be taken to mean wild horses, and so were probably synonymous, and either might be written down haphazard by the clerk as he came to the subject.) No doubt even in these early times the little horses of Exmoor were valued as hardy foundation stock from which to breed many useful sorts of steed, and certain nobles—such as William de Moine, the Comte de Montain, and the Bishop of Coutances, who all had herds of horses in other parts of the country— would encourage the keeping of these ponies on their lands.

Other sorts of horses are rarely mentioned. There are one or two references to what were probably pack-horses (*runcini*), there being one at Brendon and another at Countisbury, and mention of three riding-horses (*caballus*), two at Cutcombe and one at Almsworthy, but that is all.

LARGE ESTATES AND SMALL ONES

Once again it is to be supposed that the stock of the manor, like the land, is given collectively, and we have no means of knowing how it was apportioned. In whatever manner the flocks and herds might be made up, though, one thing strikes very forcibly: set against the area of the lands and the numbers of the peasant inhabitants, the total head of stock as given is very small indeed. A mere twelve or a score of sheep to a whole manor? Or one pack-horse between thirteen farmers? And only three riding-horses in the whole district? One simply does not believe it. It may have been said of the Domesday Book, 'Nor was there an ox, or a cow, or a swine that was not set down', but any practical farmer must disbelieve this. Then what explanation can we give? The obvious one that at once comes to mind is simple enough. The Domesday Survey was made for the express purpose of taxation. Well now, we all know what the average honest Englishman of today does with his income-tax returns: are we to suppose that our ancestors were either more honest or less worldly than ourselves? One could not hide land, of course; that was there for the commissioners to see if they rode around, but one could perhaps make it seem less valuable if the stock was scanty. If beasts were turned away to the moor or driven to the scrubby bottoms of the combes, who was going to gather them all up and count them? Alas, I am afraid we must take a good deal of fiddling for granted in the register of stock.

One last thing is worthy of note before leaving the Domesday Survey: in almost every case the tax value of the hill-country manors has increased above the pre-Conquest valuation by a considerable amount, sometimes by as much as 400 per cent (as at Countisbury, which was worth 20*s.*, and is now valued at £4). This, I believe, is in contradistinction to most other parts of the country, where the standard of agriculture had tended to decline under the impact of the Conquest. It would certainly seem as though the new landlords were here doing some hill-country reclamation to good effect.

As well as being able warriors and administrators, the Normans were zealous churchmen and church builders, and very soon all over the country small stone churches began to rise upon the sites of the earlier and simpler Saxon ones. Possibly Norman zeal was based less on deep religious faith than on the belief that the spiritual discipline of the Church would help to hold down a subject population, but be it as it may, the little Norman churches are a landmark in our country history. They are the earliest datable and truly architectural buildings that we possess, or more precisely, the earliest fragments of buildings that have come down to us. In many a moorland church, long since rebuilt in greater part, one may still find a round-headed doorway or window, perhaps blocked up, or perhaps still in use, or a font with unmistakable ornament. At Exford Old Rectory (now known as Melcombe) there is a round-headed archway still in use as a door, and if it is indeed Norman as claimed, is a very rare piece of country work, it being part of a dwelling and not of the church itself.

Exmoor can boast the remains of one Norman castle: that of Holwell, near Parracombe. This may have been raised by Martin FitzMartin soon after the Conquest, upon his acquiring the lordship of Parracombe (though there is no record of it in the Domesday Book), or it may have come into being during the troublous times of King Stephen. Today we see only the huge earthworks, for all traces of dwellings have long since vanished. There is a big 'motte' surrounded by a deep ditch or moat, and connected with this an outer courtyard or bailey. In its heyday the place would have been fortified with massive palisading upon the earthen ramparts, and there would have been a watch-tower on the motte. The hall of the lord, stables, storage, and quarters for the retainers would have been in the bailey.

Some earthworks at Bratton Fleming and at Loxhore are thought to be the remains of other castles, but they are very indefinite. Far to the east, beyond the edge of Exmoor, there was the great castle of Dunster, the stronghold of the Mohuns, but beyond the mere fact of its existence, and the influence of its lords, it hardly concerns the affairs of Exmoor.

THE ENGLISH RESURGENCE

For more than a hundred years after the Domesday survey there is darkness on the scene of history about the hills, and almost nothing to tell of how things were going with the farming folk and their homesteads in the combes. We can only guess at the bitterness under the rule of the Norman lords, and then at the resurgence of English blood and tongue that came with the twelfth century, when the people of the land had outlasted the alien rule. Then, as the twelfth century turns to the thirteenth, the light begins to come again in the form of deeds and documents and court rolls, all of them full of names of people and places. Now we see a people increasing in numbers, resurgent with life, pushing out in a fresh impetus of colonization to the still wild lands of moor and wood and tangled combe, setting small new farms wherever the ground was suitable, and fighting for home and fields, family by family, as their ancestors had first done. Everywhere the little holdings spring up, named and set for all time upon the map of western England, as enterprising man after man, sturdy farmers' sons, newly wed no doubt, seek grants from the lord of the manor to take in land upon the waste of some distant hill or make assart [1] amongst the scrub of a lonely combe. The small farms, each following the courtyard plan of before and since, take root and grow, adding field to field and more buildings as times would allow.

[1] Clearing.

Up to the days of the Black Death the movement of new settlement continued, then came at last to a halt as half the rural population was swept away by the evil pestilence. But by that time almost every farm that we know today had been established, and some others too that now have disappeared.

FARMS AND PLACE-NAMES

By the year 1300, or very soon after, we have, from the aggregate of old legal documents that have come down to us, names that sound with a familiar ring in our ears, names which despite their peculiar archaic spelling have probably changed little in their pronunciation since they were first set down in the old black-letter script upon the now stiffened parchment. They are the names of our farms, old English names all of them, some of homesteads newly made, some of settlements there before but unrecorded, some that are the original names of the Anglo-Norman manors struggling free from under the Latinization of the Domesday Book (*see* Appendix B).

Many though these familiar names are, we can be sure that there were many others too—almost every other farm that we know—but which did not have cause to get themselves documented until some later date. Indeed the fact that such are here omitted is rather to their credit, since for the most part the documents from which the above are taken are court rolls recording fines for various misdemeanours!

How eloquent are these old English names, how full of the memory of times when the western land was a wilder place, and the hill country a settler's frontier. The cotts and the combes, the leys, the worthys, the hangers, the hills, the fields, the slades, the twitchens and the bartons, they speak to us still of the land under our feet. 'Cott' or 'cote', probably the commonest of our terminations, is the homestead of the small settler, the little farm in the wilds. 'Combe' and 'hill' speak for themselves, the farms in the valley or on the hill. 'Don' or 'dun' is likewise a hill; 'down' probably derives from 'dun' which is, incidentally,

A HILL FARM IN THE MIDDLE AGES

a Celtic word. 'Ley' or 'leigh' is a clearing—newly cleared
ground. 'Field' is just field, a grass meadow. 'Hanger' is a
steep wooded hillside, a 'hanging wood'. 'Worth' or 'worthy'
is a farm or settlement, and so are 'ton' and 'ham'. 'Wood'
speaks for itself. 'Well' may mean a spring of water, or may
refer to ancient Celtic land. 'Ridge' is the crest of a hill.
'Twitchen', a not uncommon component of various Exmoor
names, derives from 'twicene', a meeting of the ways.

From these and other meanings we can guess at the origins of
many of our ancient farms. 'Kytnor' is the place of the kites,
once familiar birds on Exmoor, and Hawkwell or Hawkridge

the place of the hawks. Birchanger is the farm under the steep birch wood, Wilmersham is Wilmer's farm. Ash or Ashway or Ashton, the place of ash trees. Furzehill is the farm on the gorse-covered hill. Thornworthy is the place amongst the thorn scrub. Whitefield is probably ground thick with clover or daisies. Blackland and Blackford are either heather or bog ground—in the case of the former, which is on a dry hill, it would be the farm on the thick heather ground. Bremelridge is the bramble-covered hill. Tippercott is very likely 'Tibba's cott'. Twitchen is the farm at the fork or cross-roads. Prefixes like 'East' and 'West' or 'Higher' and 'Lower' explain themselves. So one can go on, guessing at the origin and meaning of all the old farms as one pleases.

A necessary complement to new farms was the water-mill for grinding the corn. A few mills are mentioned in Domesday Book, but most probably came into being sometime in the thirteenth century.

Whilst farms and fields were being made by vigorous peasant hands, the Church was busy too. New bits were added to the churches—the top of a tower here, a new nave or chancel there—and perhaps even a few completely rebuilt. Down in the Exe valley, on a piece of fertile and sheltered land a mile or so from Dulverton, Barlynch Priory had been founded by the Black Canons. Incidentally it is interesting to note how much land in the Exmoor country was owned by the Church in the Middle Ages; a study of ancient records shows it to be quite a large amount, much of it held by the Abbey of Neath.

THE PATTERN OF THE LAND

From the document of the perambulation of Exmoor Forest in 1298 we get the grouping, status and ownership of all the lands and manors on the Somerset side of the high moor. The names of the lords of these estates concerns us little—they had their day and are gone—but the style and description of the places are of some interest, and worth quoting (*see* Appendix B).

One feels inclined to smile at the grandiose appellation of 'vill' (township) given to so many of the places. With the exception of Porlock and Dulverton, and perhaps Winsford, hardly any can have been villages in the accepted sense. The most such places are likely to have boasted in the way of urbanization would be a church with a farm beside it (as at Stoke Pero), or a farm with a few odd cottages round about, or just two farms set together.

It is interesting to note that in almost every case each place is specified as having with it its 'woods, moors and appurtenances'. This is about the first time that any mention of the surrounding moorland has been made, and indicates that by this time at least the vast areas of waste that lay all about had been divided up among the various manors or parishes as local commonland. From the above descriptions we can draw a fair enough picture of the landscape of those times; except for the vastly greater area of moorland, and the correspondingly lesser one of fields, the countryside cannot have looked so very different from today. Farms and hamlets in a patchwork of little fields, now and again a small church tower in the midst, deep, steep wooded valleys, and all around the tawny encircling moor. So we have traced the settlement of the land from its first beginnings to its final pattern. There is much more to tell of course, but by the time at which we have now arrived, and onwards through the next five centuries until the early nineteenth century, the history of the Exmoor hill country is largely that of the Royal Forest and, as such, properly belongs to the next chapter.

3. THE DAYS OF THE ROYAL FOREST

About the beginning of the thirteenth century, at that period when the pattern of England was emerging from under the shock of the Norman Conquest, we are for the first time made aware that the whole of the wild heart of Exmoor, and much of the surrounding country as well, is claimed by the Crown as a Royal Forest.

How and when this first came about is uncertain, but possibly this state of things evolved towards the end of the last Saxon, or Anglo-Danish, period, after the country had developed into a more or less centralized kingdom. That the proclaiming of 'forests' was a pre-Conquest measure is amply borne out by various pieces of evidence, though not until after the coming of the Normans did the 'forest' bounds become so wide and the governing laws so severe.

What, one may fairly ask, was a Royal Forest, and how could land be so claimed, and why? Looking back in history, as far as one can, one may say that most probably it all began round about the time when the first flare of Anglo-Saxon invasion and settlement had passed and the kingdom, or kingdoms, of the English had become established, and some sort of recognized government and machinery of law set up. Now all land not yet settled and claimed by individuals or village communities would be regarded as the general property of the state, and vested in the person of the king as the head of the state. The next most obvious thing would be that these 'wastes'—in many cases great tracts of moorland, forest and mountain—would form the natural refuge or harbouring-ground of all the wild creatures that had been driven from the more settled parts. With the Saxon princes, as with all dynasties of vigour, hunting was a passion, providing them with both sport and delicious meats, hence it would be but one step from the nominal possession of the wild lands and their beasts to the desire for the complete ownership and preservation thereof. So ultimately it would come about that an area rich in game would be declared a 'Royal Forest' and all the beasts therein the personal property of the king. A Royal Forest was therefore what today we would call a 'game reserve', an area within which all wild creatures in general, and certain sorts in particular, were especially preserved for the benefit of the king.

(There is of course another aspect to this which it is only fair to mention. In early times, when many predatory wild beasts inhabited the woods and wilder parts, it was the duty of princes and overlords to hunt these down and so protect their dependants' lives and property. Hunting, like war, was the proper occupation of the strong and the mighty. However, by historical times hunting had become a princely passion, and it was the preservation rather than the extermination of wild creatures that was aimed at.)

However, we hear little or nothing about these forests until after the Norman Conquest, and then we hear very much indeed. All the Norman kings and their Angevin successors were fierce and inveterate hunters, and each of them, from William the Conqueror to King John, seized upon and enlarged the forests to the greatest possible extent, perhaps even created new ones, and enacted savage laws to govern all within.

THE FOREST OF EXMOOR

Apart from the brief reference in the Domesday Book to Dodo, Almar and Godric of Withypool, who are specified as foresters, there is nothing especially concerning the Forest of Exmoor until the year 1219, when a perambulation of the bounds of the forest were made in the name of the king, the young Henry III.

Exmoor Forest was probably put 'in regard' (i.e. its status and bounds officially proclaimed), by Henry II. It was in 1184 that Henry II issued the famous 'Assize of Woodstock'—beginning, 'this is the Assize of our Lord Henry the King, son of Matilda, in England, concerning his forest and his hunting . . .'—which great landmark of Anglo-Norman forest law brought huge areas of country under a code that had its own courts and justices, and which meted out savage punishments for trivial offences.

King John, like his predecessors a tireless and insatiable hunter, went further and afforested still more land, even to the extent of proclaiming the whole of Devon to be forest. Such tyranny, however, was more than his subjects could stand, and by the terms of the Magna Carta he was forced to promise the disafforestation of all lands unlawfully declared by him as forest.

In 1217, early in the reign of Henry III, the notable *Carta de Foresta* was first promulgated, the purpose of which was to disafforest lands unlawfully declared forest, and to re-establish the proper bounds of the remaining forest areas. All this took a long time, despite the fact that a commission was appointed in 1219, and the subsequent perambulations of the forests did not take place until 1278 and 1298.

Exmoor was one of the five ancient Royal Forests of Somerset, the other four being Petherton, Neroche, Mendip and Selwood. Incidentally the term 'forest' has been the cause of a good deal of misunderstanding of the true nature of Exmoor. Through long association and common usage the word has become synonymous for extensive natural woodland, and thus has led people to suppose that all the old Royal Forests were heavily wooded. Many of them were—such as Sherwood and the New Forest—but others, notably Exmoor and Dartmoor, never had any trees upon their heights, and were always by nature bare and windswept. (The word 'forest' probably derived from *foras*, 'outside', meaning land outside of ordinary ownership and law.) It is this barren character of high Exmoor that undoubtedly led King John to annex the lands of Culbone, Yarnor, Worthy, Porlock, Bossington, Doverhay, Hawkcombe, Lucott, Buckethole, Holnicote, Luccombe, Stoke Pero, Wilmersham, Cloutsham, Dunkery, Elsworthy, Style, Walland, Hawkwell, Cutcombe, Quarm, Exford, Winsford, Howe, Withycombe, Edbrook, Exton, Withypool, Landacre, Hawkridge, Ashway, Liscombe, Cawkett, Hawkwell, Dulverton and Barlynch, and to include them unlawfully within the bounds of Exmoor Forest. Then, as now, these were the regions of the thick scrub-oak woods and deep tangled combes where the red deer harboured, and loved to be, and whence they might be roused on a hunting morning. When the king was forced to disgorge these ill-gotten lands, he lost the best deer-covers of the Exmoor country.

PERAMBULATIONS OF EXMOOR

The Exmoor perambulation of 1279 was carried out by twelve knights of the county of Somerset, assisted by the foresters and verderers, and the bounds of the forest were declared to run thus: beginning at 'Cornestake' (Cosgate, now County Gate), the bounds go by 'Fifstake' (an ancient mark of some sort round about the head of Deddycombe), as far as 'Hauekescumbesheved' (Hawkcombe Head), then 'by the top of the hill' to 'Osmundesburghwey' (Aldermans Barrow), then by 'little Dexe' (Little Exe—Alcombe Water?), to 'Great Dexe' (the River Exe) and thence as far as 'la Roode' (Road Castle). From 'la Roode' to 'Hernesbureghe' (Hernsbarrow—an ancient barrow on Room Hill), 'by the great way' (an ancient highway coming up by Road Castle), and on by this to 'Wamburegh' (Wambarrow—the barrows on the summit of Winsford Hill), and to 'Langestone' (Longstone—the Caractacus Stone) and to 'Magil . . . heued' (Mounsey Hill Gate); thence 'by the great way' between the two 'Esseweyes' (the two Ashway farms) to the waters of the 'Burewelle' (River Barle), and along the water to where the 'Danesbrok' (Danesbrook) falls into the 'Buregel' (the Barle at Castle Bridge); from this point back to Cosgate by way of the county boundary.

By this perambulation the parishes of Withypool and Hawkridge, together with parts of Exford and Winsford, were retained within the Royal Forest, but all the other lands aforementioned were put out of the forest, as were all those lands on the Devonshire side which may have been accounted forest by King John.

However, this definition apparently did not satisfy, for a second perambulation took place later in the same year. Possibly the inhabitants of Withypool, Hawkridge and Exford had protested—after all, 'a fifteenth part of the movable goods of all England' had been paid to the Crown by the people of the realm in order to secure the charters of the forest and of common liberties, and as liberty had cost them dear they were no doubt determined to have it.

The second perambulation began this time at 'Wyveleford' (Willingford) and the bounds were declared thus: from Willingford in a straight line to the 'Hockstone' (Hocklestone—a stone where Muddy Lane Gate now stands), from thence in a straight line to 'Shyreburnesse' (Sheardon Hutch), and so down the river to 'Langakre' (Landacre) 'leaving that within the forest', then straight to 'Stonhuste' (a stone that must have existed somewhere at the head of the little combe that has always marked the boundary of Landacre on the east); from 'Stonhuste' to the 'Dermark' (possibly the small barrow with the white stone in the middle of Bradymoor), thence to 'She . . . combeshevede' (Shutcombe Head), to 'la Rydeforde' (Redford—a ford somewhere in the upper Pennycombe above Asholt), up to 'Rodestone' (Redstone—on the Exford–Simonsbath road), straight to the 'Exe', then in a straight line up 'Spraccombediche' (Orchard Bottom and Spracombe) to

'Spraccombeshiede (Spracombe Head—near Larkbarrow Corner); from there in a straight line to 'Osmundesbergwe' (Aldermans Barrow), then in a straight line to 'Blakeborgh' (Black Barrow), again in a straight line to 'Lillescombesset' (the point where the Lillycombe stream runs into Weir Water at Robbers Bridge), up the stream to 'Lyllecumbeshevede' (Lillycombe Head), 'by the highway' to 'Fistones' (above Deddycombe), then to 'Cornesgate' (Cosgate), and then down 'by a ditch' to the 'Ar' (Oare) River which is on the county boundary; thence by the 'metes and bounds' of Devon and Somerset back to Willingford.

By this second perambulation the whole of Exford, Winsford and Hawkridge were disafforested, and all of Withypool except the manor of Landacre. To the north, the last of the Porlock lands were relinquished, leaving only Oare within the forest.

A third perambulation was made in 1298, nearly twenty years later, though for what specific purpose is not clear, for the bounds are given (with some variations of spelling) exactly as before (i.e. in the second circuit). This perambulation began and ended at Cosgate. One thing, though, seems contradictory: in an appended list of all the local lands and manors of Somerset, now outside the bounds and disafforested, the manor of Landacre is named, and so is no longer within the forest. Since the bounds at this point are still given as 'Deresmarke' to 'Stonehiste', and so to the Barle, the only conclusion is that the boundary was diverted to run from Stonehiste across Bradymoor to Sheardon Hutch. (Unless, of course, in the first place Stonhuste or Stonehiste was not the head of the combe—the name would seem to indicate 'place of stones', and the scattered white stones to the west of Bradymoor at once spring to mind—but some place farther west, and likewise the Deermark, a more westerly point.) Anyway, the relationship of Landacre to the forest has always been somewhat uncertain.

Yet another perambulation seems to have been made in 1300 following the same bounds and confirming them, the only variant being that the actual circuit began and ended at Willingford. Incidentally in none of these perambulations are the bounds of the forest on the western side precisely described. It is merely stated that they follow the line of the county boundary. From this one can only deduce that either the county border was considered to be so well known as to need no further specification, or else that it was at this time so vague as to be indeterminate, and that the commissioners just took the easiest course and made a sweeping statement to save themselves further trouble.

Subsequent to this it would seem that the King (Edward I) made some attempt to regain the disafforested portions, both here and about other forests, but generally without success. All through the Middle Ages the relationship between monarch and people was sorely strained by the matter of the Royal Forests, the wide extent of which—even after the implementation of the Charter of the Forest—were the cause of continuous resentment.

As to the Forest of Exmoor, we now see it, except for the parish of Oare, reduced to the wild uninhabited heart of the high moor. As already mentioned, it was notably treeless, so much so that the only two trees ever known within its bounds— the Hoar Oak and Kite Oak (Kittuck)—were for generations well-known landmarks. The disafforestation of all the surrounding lands with their deep wooded combes had shorn it of the best deer-covers, but still it was of value to the Crown, and was to be held for many centuries to come. With regard to Oare, there seems to be no record of the date of its disafforestation, but very probably it was put out of the forest soon after the last mentioned perambulation.

FOREST LAW

That the folk of the countryside should desire to be free of the forest bounds and the forest law one can readily understand. Forest law was harsh and restrictive in every way, and in early medieval times was enforced with barbarous cruelty. From the days of the Normans until the year 1217—when the Charter of the Forest was wrung from the Crown—any man who slew a deer or any other wild creature within the forest might be hanged, blinded or otherwise mutilated in punishment. After 1217, however, the penalty was commuted to a fine, though a very stiff one. No doubt the Crown found that after all there was some profit to be made out of fines, whereas none was to be had from the mutilation of a wretched offender.

The laws of the forest were framed especially to give the utmost protection to the beasts therein. The principal 'beasts of the forest' were red deer (stag and hind), the fallow deer (buck and doe) and the wild boar, though roe and hare were also included. Of them all, it was the big red deer stag, the 'hart', that was the greatest, the noblest creature, the royal beast, the delight of kings, the quarry of princes. He it was who was lord of the forest, for whom all things were done, all provisions made, and whose red-gold body excited the desire of prince and poacher alike.

BEASTS OF THE FOREST

The native wild red deer were the beasts of venison of Exmoor. Fallow deer do not seem to have inhabited the forest at any time in a wild state. Whether the roe ever existed here is uncertain—there is, however, one solitary mention of 'caprioles' in an ancient forest document, which would seem to refer to roe deer. Wild boar probably existed in the earlier Middle Ages (tusks of a wild boar have, I believe, been found on Withypool Hill, though of what date is not known), but would seem to have become extinct by the time we get any documentary forest evidence.

OFFICERS OF THE FOREST

For the management of the forest and enforcement of its laws, a number of officials were appointed. Chief of these was the

Keeper of the Forest, Forester-in-fee, or Warden, a person of high rank into whose hands the keeping of the forest was given by the king. The office could be, and largely was, an hereditary one. He or she—for on one occasion the keeping of Exmoor passed into the hands of a woman, Sabina Pecche—might appoint a deputy if they so wished.

For a woman to hold such an office in the stern and warlike Middle Ages was very unusual, and one would like to know more about Sabina Pecche. Unfortunately little or nothing is known about her, nor likely to be now. All that the records tell us is that she inherited the wardenship from her brother, Richard de Plessy, she being his heiress, and held it until her death in 1308. Her husband, Nicholas Pecche, seems to have been invested as her deputy.

Next in importance were the verderers. These were the judicial officers of the forest, sworn to maintain its laws, and to them had to be brought all charges and complaints.

Then came the foresters. These were the equivalent of the modern gamekeeper, whose duties were to watch over the deer and other game and also the 'vert' or herbage of the forest, and to apprehend poachers and other wrongdoers. One gathers that these foresters were generally disliked and regarded with hostility by the country folk, for obvious reasons, and complaints were frequently made against them that they exceeded their duty, and took advantage of their position to oppress the ordinary folk who lived in or around the forest.

At a later date one hears of officials called rangers, but just what their position and duties might be is not certain. Possibly they acted as masters of any arrangements made for hunting, when some prince or noble came to hunt in the forest. We first hear of a ranger of Exmoor during the sixteenth century, in the reign of Queen Elizabeth I, and here the term seems to be synonymous with warden.

Regarders were independent men appointed for the making of a 'regard' or periodic survey of the forest. They were principally concerned with any encroachment upon the territory of the forest, such as the unlawful making of enclosures or felling of timber, and they had to report on the general state of things within the forest bounds, which report was made to the justices in eyre at the next sessions.

Agisters were officials whose duty was to deal with the agisting or depasturing of stock within the forest, and to collect and record the dues therefrom. There seems to be no record of agisters in connection with Exmoor, so one may assume that here the work was done by the ordinary foresters.

Woodwards were men appointed to care for and report on those woods within a forest that were privately owned. The woodward had to be appointed by the owner of the wood, but he was answerable to the authorities for the state of the wood. Here again, the importance of the woods as deer-covert is seen. A list of the woods and woodwards for the Forest of Exmoor exists, dated 1275. These woods are named as follows: 'Wyneford' (Winsford), 'Haukerigge' (Hawkridge), 'Asweye' (Ashway), 'Wydepole' (Withypool), 'Stoke' (Stoke Pero), 'Porlock' (Porlock and Oare), 'Dovery' (Doverhay), 'Bugedehole' (Buckethole), 'Lege' (Ley), 'Arnor' (Horner), 'Wymeresham' (Wilmersham), 'Amundeswerthe' (Almsworthy), 'Claudesham' (Cloutsham), 'Lucumbe' (Luccombe), 'Hanecombe' (Hannycombe), 'Nordecumbe' (Northcombe), 'Hauekeswelle' (Hawkwell), 'Tolchet' (Cawkett) and 'Dulvertone' (Dulverton).

All these woods, however, were put outside of the forest by the perambulation of 1278.

Offences under forest law would seem generally to fall into one of two categories: offences against the venison and against the vert. The former consisted of those acts that were directly harmful to the beasts of the forest—the killing of deer or other creatures, the pursuing or disturbing of them, the unlawful possession of greyhounds or any large dogs that had not been 'lawed' (a cruel practice whereby a dog's feet were maimed so that it could not run properly), or the keeping of bows and arrows. The latter consisted of such things as were harmful to the cover and herbage of the forest—the felling of trees, the making of enclosures, the cutting of turf, the unlawful pasturing of animals, etc.

All offences were doubly serious when they took place in the 'fence month' or forbidden month. This was a period of thirty-one days at midsummer, from the middle of June to the middle of July, and was intended to extend over that time of the year when the hinds were calving. During this period all things that might possibly disturb them were expressly forbidden. Animals, particularly pigs, might not be pastured in the forest, no man might leave the highway, and extra vigilance was observed in all things.

The Courts of the Forest were the Court of Attatchement, held every forty days, at which the verderers heard cases and committed offenders to trial at the Forest Eyre; the Court of Swainmote, held three times a year, and concerned mainly with local rights and privileges; the Court of Regard, held every three years, dealing with overall matters of the forest; and the Eyre of the Forest, the supreme court, held intermittently at some county town, and presided over by the Justices in Eyre. This last tried and punished all offenders against the Forest Law.

POACHERS AND POACHING

Despite the severe penalties that might be incurred, the urge and instinct to poach was strong in the hearts of the country folk. In seasons when things were hard and meat was scarce, the temptation aroused by the sight of a fine young deer in the bracken was often more than could be borne. And as to lesser matters, such as the various offences against the 'vert', the men of Exmoor probably showed as scant respect to the bureaucracy of that time as they do to its manifestations today.

The several rolls of the Forest Eyres and Inquisitions concerning Exmoor, which still exist, and which collectively date from

1257 to 1376, make homely reading, and in their list of offences call to mind things and scenes and places as though from yesterday: William Herlewyne and three companions have killed a stag in Hawkridge wood and have carried away the carcase, but William cannot be found, and so he is outlawed. John the Parson of Hawkridge has 'assarted' four acres of ground, which he has sown once with winter corn and thrice with spring corn. Elias of Zeal has taken-in two acres, James of Hill has taken one acre and sown it with corn and oats. Warine de Secchevile has 'wasted' the wood of Oare. Hillary de Munceaus has cut down trees in Ashway wood. Geoffrey of Buttery in North Molton has found within the forest a stag shot dead with an arrow, and has taken the carcase away himself. Huge of Luccombe is detained in prison because he is a noted poacher. Thomas de Tracy and his men have roused a stag 'within the liberty of the County of Devon' and hunted him into the forest and taken him at Hawkridge, and have carried away the venison to the house of Huge de Tracy at Tawstock. Thomas Gourt in Molland and William Wyme of Bremley have entered the forest with bows and arrows, and have shot a hind and chased and taken her in Langcombe, and carried away the venison to their houses in Molland, and the thing has been done with the knowledge and help of the parson of Hawkridge. John Scrutenger of Cloutsham has taken a hind during Pentecost and carried the carcase to Cloutsham. Richard of Furzehill has taken a calf in the fence-month and carried it to his house; Henry of Bonington and some others have taken a calf which they saw stray from the forest. John of Cloutsham has killed another hind, this time with the connivance of the parson of Oare. Richard Beaumund 'of the County of Devon', with Molyns his huntsman, Viger of Clayhanger, and Beyven the Tailor are noted poachers and have taken many stags and hinds. Huge of Landacre has taken-in a meadow outside Landacre, and is ordered to give up the land. Adam of Newland, Hameline of Blackland and some others of Withypool have cut peat without warrant. Henry of

Oare has shot two stags in the fence-month and carried away the venison. Richard le Webbe and some others have set fire to the moor and have thereby burnt a thousand acres of heath upon the forest. The rector of Oare has felled some oak saplings and carried the wood away for his own purposes. The Abbot of Cleeve and various other gentry with lands about the moor have been in the habit of pasturing their cattle within the forest without warrant for the same. Henry of Oare has shot a stag on Long Hoccombe. Henry of Gatcombe, near Molland, has shot a stag which he found grazing in his rye. Richard of Lucott has fired Lucott moor, and the flames have leapt to the heath of the forest, and again the king's heather is burnt, this time a hundred acres. William of Oare and his tenants have been digging turf for fuel without warrant. Robert Corun, knight, has taken in Barrow wood at Winsford a stag from the forest whose 'peace had been proclaimed'. The same Sir Robert Corun has killed another stag in Dulverton woods, where and at what time he purported to be hunting foxes. So the entries go on, and for every offence recorded and punished one may guess at a score or a hundred undetected and 'got away with'.

MEDIEVAL HUNTING

With all this care for the preservation and wellbeing of the deer and the maintenance of the Royal Forest, one may wonder and fairly ask, did the kings of England ever actually come in person to hunt upon Exmoor? No definite answer can be given to this, one way or another, for no documentary record of any such occasion exists, but from certain odd bits of evidence one might guess that they probably did in early times.

The Saxon kings, who were much in the West Country, are said to have maintained a residence—a hunting-box no doubt— at Porlock, and certainly the description of the hunting incident in the tale of Edmund and Dunstan, though presumably set at

66

Cheddar, could very well be matched at Glenthorn upon the Exmoor cliffs: Edmund the King is out hunting the deer with his hounds and they are laid on to a big stag. Then at last the hounds are running in view, and about to come up with their deer, and he in desperation heads for the edge of the cliffs. The king, with thoughts only for the chase, is riding well up on a hard-mouthed horse, and sees not the danger. At the very moment that the hounds come up with the stag he goes over the cliff, taking the pack with him to destruction. Edmund is close behind, he sees the cliff edge but cannot stop his madly excited horse and, in facing doom, like many another man, thinks in a flash of his recent sins and of his quarrel with Dunstan. He cries out that if God will spare his life he will make his peace with Dunstan. Then the horse struggles to stop itself on the falling ground and manages finally to come to a halt on the very brink of the giddy drop. Such a tale could be paralleled in more than one incident with the Devon and Somerset Stag-hounds of our own time.

The fact that the early Angevin kings incorporated so many of the parishes of north Devon and west Somerset into the Forest of Exmoor, and even tried to subject all Devon to Forest Law, would seem to suggest that this was one of their favoured hunting districts. In various documents of the thirteenth century several estates in Devon are specified as being held on the condition of certain formal services being rendered 'on the King's coming into Exemore to hunt'. King John was much in Somerset, at Wells, Taunton and at Bridgewater, where he had a castle, and it would be strange if, tireless and insatiable hunter that he was, he did not frequently visit his Forest of Exmoor.

Whether or no the king came often or seldom to his West Country forests, there is sure to have been hunting and the cry of the hounds upon the heights of Exmoor through all the centuries. The king might grant the right to hunt in his forest to one or other of his nobles, the right to hunt deer to one person, and the right to hunt other creatures to someone else. The de Moines or Mohuns, the Lords of Dunster, were allowed the right—sometimes, at least—to hunt deer on Exmoor, for in the Forest Eyre roll of 1257 it is recorded that Reynold de Mohun took in the forest four stags and three roebucks 'by writ of the Lord King'. A few other instances of the hunting of Exmoor deer under warrant have also come down to us, such as the right of Roger la Zuche to have two stags by gift of the king (1237), or Hugh Durburgh to have one hind in February 1376. Also, certain persons of high rank, such as bishops, earls and barons, might, on passing through the forest, lawfully kill one or two deer on their way—hunting *en route*, as it were. After 1508, when the forest was leased to its wardens, the latter were entitled to keep hounds and hunt the deer as their right, but prior to this they seem not to have had any such privilege except by special grant.

It is a matter of interest that Edward, Duke of York, grandson of Edward III, author of that first English book of hunting, *The Master of Game* (written some time between 1402 and 1413), was married to Philippa de Mohun, second daughter of Lady Joan de Mohun of Dunster Castle. Philippa herself held the manor of Cutcombe-Mohun as her share of the Mohun estates, which lands ran right up to Dunkery and the Forest of Exmoor. It is not unreasonable to suppose, therefore, that this royal duke and his wife frequently came to hunt upon Exmoor. Anyone who has read those pages of *The Master of Game* devoted to stag hunting must surely feel that here is a man who has seen a great stag roused in the woods under Dunkery, has heard the hounds crying in the combes and the horns echoing from the hillsides, has known all the ruses of the stag in covert and stream, and has seen him stand at bay in some rocky pool under the moor.

A further note of interest is the mention in the old records, in two instances, of 'a stag whose peace had been proclaimed'. This refers to the custom whereby a stag who had been roused in the forest and hunted beyond its bounds, and eventually lost in the outer country, was then 'proclaimed' by public announcement, i.e. folk were forbidden to harm such a stag, even though he was now outside the forest, and he was to be left in peace to return at will to the forest. A stag that had been so hunted and lost by the sovereign or a prince of the royal blood was termed 'a hart royal proclaimed'.

In the case of beasts other than deer, licences to hunt in the Royal Forests were freely granted to such nobles as were in favour with the king. At various dates between 1227 and 1285, no less than ten notable persons received the right to hunt with their own hounds upon Exmoor and in the other forests of Somerset. The Bishop of Bath had the right to hunt all beasts except stag, hind, buck and doe; Reynold de Mohun to hunt hare, fox, cat and badger; William de Avenell to hunt hare, fox and cat. Roger de Cantilupe to hunt hare, fox and cat; Ralph de Bakepuz to hunt hare, fox, cat, squirrel and badger; Roger de Thoney to hunt hare, fox, cat and badger; Hugh Everard, Canon of Wells, to hunt hare, fox, badger and cat; Laurence de Sancto Mauro to hunt fox, hare, badger and cat; Alan de Plogenet to hunt fox and hare; Alan de Plunkenet to hunt fox and hare.

We can easily picture a hunting-party of those far-off days, hearing again their voices and catching a glimpse of the hunting-green of their clothes as they come through the trees on their way up the combe—they pass a break in the scrub and we see them clearly now—the gentlefolk proud-faced on their sturdy horses, the gleam of gilded buckles on heavy, coloured leather harness, the flash of hunting-knife and spear, and now the varlets on foot with the hounds in couples, heavy, ponderous, dewlapped brutes for slowly working out a line, slender greyhounds for running a quarry in view, perhaps a mastiff or two for pulling down a wounded beast. They talk and laugh and brush through the bracken and are gone, and the horses' hooves clink on the stones on the higher path. Good hunting to you, men of another age, for your sport is ours still, though manners and customs change.

GRAZING RIGHTS

As the Middle Ages moved on, the Royal Forests in general, and Exmoor in particular, began to have, in addition to their primary purpose as hunting-grounds, another and more commercial use. Within so large a natural area there were automatically immense stretches of grazing-ground and forage far in excess of the needs of the deer that harboured there, and such ground offered ready pasturage to large numbers of domestic stock of all sorts. The Crown was not slow to see that a profit, amounting to a revenue, could be had from the agisting of stock within the forest. The custom of depasturing at certain seasons of the year, upon the payment of some fee or due, large numbers of animals from the surrounding farms and villages, seems to have obtained from very early times. At first such stocking would have been very secondary in importance to the preservation of wild game for hunting, but gradually as time went on, and the kings of England abode at Windsor and came seldom or never to their outlying western forests, these vast demesnes came to be looked upon more and more as huge areas of summer pasturing, and less and less as specific hunting reserves—a natural return to, or continuance of, the ancient practice of taking the flocks and herds up to the high hills for the summer months. Perhaps the custom had never ceased, but had merely been appropriated by the Crown, for by the time we have records and details of the agisting, we find various sorts of people claiming pasturage in the forest as a right. Perhaps it had always been so, ever since the Bronze Age men moved up to the hills in the month of May.

From this practice of agistment many customs, rights and dues grew up. By the sixteenth century we find the customs and rules of the pasturing of Exmoor thoroughly established and, though most of the relative documents date from this or subsequent periods, there is little doubt that this recognized state of things had been so 'since the memory of man runneth not to the contrary'.

FREE SUITORS

Those who claimed the right of pasture within the Forest fell into two classes: the Free Suitors and the Suitors-at-Large. The Free Suitors were the men of the fifty-two Free Suit tenements of Withypool and Hawkridge, and they occupied a peculiar and privileged position amongst the folk of the moor, having rights upon the forest for which they paid no money dues, but rendering instead certain personal services. Just how or why the men of Withypool and its sister parish, and they alone, should have come to be so bound in association with the Royal Forest is not known, but it is to be remembered that these two parishes remained wholly within the forest bounds to a slightly later date than others, and very probably may have been an integral part of the Forest from very ancient times.

The fifty-two Free Suits were attached to the ancient farms of the district in varying numbers. The earliest existing Suitors' Roll, which dates only from 1797, but which probably records things as they had been from very ancient times, gives us the list of farms and their suits (*see* Appendix C).

The rights of the Free Suitors were: free pasturage within the forest for sheep (in ancient times 140 for the day time only, they having to be driven out again at night, but in later times they might be 'leared', i.e. lie there all the while); horses (five horses, mares or colts, not counting foals); cattle (as many as they could overwinter in their own farms); pigs (originally one sow and her piglets, two pigs under two years old and one pig under three years old, but after the sixteenth century the pasturing of pigs seems to have ceased). The right to cut and carry away as much turf, heath and fern as they could themselves consume on their tenements. The right to fish in the rivers of the forest and those about their own tenements.

71

Exemption from jury service at the assizes. Freedom to buy and sell at the markets without toll.

THE SWAINMOTE COURTS

In return for these rights they had to perform the following duties: to do suit and service at the two Exmoor courts (the Swainmotes) held each year; to 'drive' the forest on horseback nine times a year upon lawful warning from the forester: five times for horses (three times in summer and twice in winter), three times for cattle (twice before 25th July and once after that if called upon), and once for sheep (for 'wool' or unshorn sheep nine days before midsummer); to perambulate the forest bounds once in seven years; to serve on the jury of the coroner's inquest when any dead body was found within the forest.

On the occasions of driving the forest, each suitor or his deputy had to turn up mounted on a good horse. The starting-point for the drift was Wiccombe or Wincombe Head, upon Bradymoor, at the place where the last of the Landacre enclosures drop away. The riders assembled at daybreak and the only valid excuses a suitor could make for not turning up were that 'his wife be in travail with child', or that they had 'laid their dow to leven to be baked that day'. The cattle and sheep to be rounded up were such as had been depastured there, but the 'horse beasts' or 'widge beasts' would mostly be the little almost wild Exmoor ponies whose home the high hills had been since time immemorial. The animals rounded up were driven down to the forest pound at Withypool for impounding and claiming, and the drift itself would seem to have taken some eight to ten hours—comparatively quick time for the job, one would say, considering the vast area to be covered, and all the innumerable combes and wild rough places to be drawn. There must have been good team work amongst these men of Withypool and Hawkridge, and hard riding to boot.

The periodic perambulation rides were of course to define and make remembered the old forest bounds. The suitors rode,

DRIVING THE FOREST IN ANCIENT TIMES

I believe, in a long string, nose to tail, keeping exactly to the boundary line, so that no part or point should be forgotten, and stopping at each of the recognized stone marks to emphasize that particular point.

The Suitors-at-Large were the representatives of those other manors and townships about the moor, and the freeholders of the lands thereabouts, who also claimed right of pasture, but who had to pay a money-due for the privilege.

All the matters of agisting, rights and privileges, and the business arising therefrom, were dealt with by the Swainmote

Courts. Two of these courts were held annually, both it would seem in the open air. The first took place at Landacre on the morning after Ascension Day, and was held in the fields just above the bridge (there are two fields there still called by the name of the Court Hams). The second assembled in Hawkridge churchyard on the morning of the Friday of Pentecost, and then adjourned to Withypool to sit somewhere by the pound. To these courts had to come the forest officers, the Free Suitors, the Suitors-at-Large with their 'hands' and their branding-irons, the lords of the manors or their bailiffs and any other landowners concerned. A lawyer, appointed by the warden, presided over the court, and managed proceedings

At such a court the proceedings would open with a roll call of the suitors, and those not present would have a fine attached. Then a jury would be empanelled from amongst the Free Suitors, and the assorted business begun. There would be the presentment of all manner of petty wrongdoings, such as trespass, theft or improper impounding of stock and infringement of rules, and the fixing of fines thereto. There would be arguments about the various rights—as, for instance, the persistent claim of the men of North Molton to *free* pasturage— and the prices to be paid by 'strangers' for the pasturing of their beasts. (Outsiders also might have stock agisted on the forest, but they had to pay twice the rate fixed for the suitors.) The court would presently adjourn for what was undoubtedly the highlight of the day: the free refreshments provided at the expense of the warden. (One hopes the weather was fine.) Sometimes there were other diversions. At the Hawkridge Court of 1580, one Peter Edgecombe, having some grievance against Sir John Poyntz, the then warden, stormed into the assembly, accompanied by William Nethercott and some others, all 'arrayed in warlike manner with weapons, coats of mail and defence, pistols charged, swords, bucklers, daggers, and other weapons as well . . .', and demanded that the proceedings stop and Edgecombe himself preside. It is to be gathered that not many of the folk present remained to argue in the face of such armament and 'other weapons as well'— they just went home as fast as they could.

CATTLE AND SHEEP

The 'custom of the forest' for agisting was that each spring men were sent by the forester into the local market towns to make proclamation of the prices at which they would take sheep, cattle and horses for that year's pasturing. The principal places for 'crying the moor' were Barnstaple, South Molton, North Molton, Combe Martin, Dunster and Porlock. When the beasts were brought up to be turned into the forest, the forester checked the numbers and marks of each contingent, and these were entered in the 'Forest Book'. Sheep were put into the forest in March or May, and remained there until shearing time, when they had to be driven down and taken home by their owners. 'Tellers' were appointed to count out the sheep as they left the forest, and any unauthorized creatures were charged for at double rates. Most of the sheep came in from North Devon, and there was one 'telling-house' at Span Head, and another at Hoarook, the remains of which can still be seen a little way up the water. The drift made by the Free Suitors 'nine days before Midsummer' was to gather up any sheep left behind after the telling out, and these were driven down to the pound by the bridge at Withypool. Such sheep had to be claimed by their owners within a certain period or they were forfeit to the forester. After shearing, all accredited sheep might return to the forest until about the end of October.

Cattle would go out to the forest from May to October. Drifts were made two or three times in the summer upon notice being given by the forester to the Free Suitors on the preceding night. Horses it seems might stay upon the forest either for the summer, or all the year round, according to payment. They were 'driven for' up to five times in the year. Unclaimed cattle and horses were kept at Withypool in a field beside the pound (which was near the bridge on the south bank of the river) for a year and a day, after which they were forfeit as strays.

About the end of the sixteenth century the numbers of beasts depastured annually upon Exmoor were estimated at 40,000 sheep, 1,000 head of cattle and 400 horses. The wide high moor, a sea of yellow summer sedge and grass, unbroken by any hedge, dotted with herds of grazing beasts, must then have resembled a rolling prairie land. Cowboy country indeed—a land of galloping hooves and tossing horns, and beasts running before the shouting of riders on horseback.

Meanwhile the great days of the Elizabethan age had come to the West Country, bringing with them a resurgence of life, enterprise and adventure, and a revival of agriculture.

Looking back to the fourteenth century, we find the visitation of the Black Death (1347–8), which killed off about half the rural population, called a halt to the colonizing of the hill country and the carving out of new farms. Indeed it seems probable that after this calamity many of the little 'new made farmsteads' went down again—as, for instance, we know from certain evidence that there were once three Brightworthys (Higher, Middle and Lower), and two Landacres (Higher and Lower) where now there stand only single farms with no trace of any others.

The recovery of farming after this dreadful happening was slow and very gradual. In many parts of the country sheep replaced corn over wide areas, as needing so much less labour than arable crops, and ultimately much prosperity was brought to England from the resulting wool trade. Exmoor, mainly pastoral from the first, would hardly notice such a changeover. The sheep would increase a little more, the corn become a little less, otherwise things would go on much as before.

ELIZABETHAN AFFLUENCE—A NEW FARMHOUSE

THE ELIZABETHAN ERA

By the sixteenth century the population had increased again, and at the same time wonderful discovery of the New World opened new vistas and provided new impetus for the West Country. The west, hitherto the 'back-of-beyond' to the more prosperous regions of England, was now in the forefront of progress and adventure, looking out from all its ports and harbours to the promise of the Americas beyond the ocean. The spirit of the age, coupled with the need for more produce, caused a fresh upsurge of agricultural pioneering and general interest in farming which reached even the remote hill-country regions.

In the moorland country new works of reclamation were undertaken, new enclosures made, old farms rebuilt. Many a fine old farmhouse that stands today under the shadow of the moor had its origin in the busy years between the accession of Queen Elizabeth and the death of James I. The typical farmhouse of the period was one in which one entered, through a slope-roofed porch, into a passage, to the right or left of which was the general living-room kitchen with its huge fireplace and attached bread-oven. This chimney breast was usually set on the side of the house next to the porch, and its tall massive chimney soared high above the long thatched roof. Beyond the living-room there was usually a parlour or withdrawing-room, and if one was very grand and well off there might be a separate kitchen, usually on the other side of the passageway, where the hired hands had their meals. On the north side there would be a large cool dairy. A cupboard-stair somewhere behind a latched door gave access to the bedrooms above, low ceilinged under the roof timbers. This was the general pattern, with slight variations, which persisted to the end of the eighteenth century. The house still faced inwards (almost always south or south-east) towards the courtyard, for possible defence still had to be thought of in a country lacking a police force or other general means of maintaining law and order.

New bridges too were built, in many places where there had hitherto been only fords. These carried the trains of packhorses dry shod over the rushing streams, as they trotted on their way to the markets laden with the increased produce of the farms, or returned with craft goods of the townships.

Leland, the antiquary and topographer, touring the West Country between 1538 and 1540, gives us the first written description of Exmoor that has come down to us. He says:

'From Dunster to Exford village a seven mile. Of these seven miles three or four of the first were all hilly and rocky, full of brooks in every hill's bottom and meetly wooded . . . the residue of the way to Exford was partly on a moor and somewhat barren of corn, partly hilly, having many brooks gathering to the hither ripe of Exe river. There is a little timber bridge at Exford over Exe brook, there being a small water. . . . From Exford to Simonsbath bridge a four miles all by Forest, barren and moorish ground, where is store and breeding of young cattle, but little or no corn or habitation. There runneth at this place called Simonsbath a river betwixt two great moorish hills in a deep bottom and there is a bridge of wood over this water. The water in summer most commonly runneth flat upon stones easy to be passed over, but when rains come and storms of winter it rageth and is deep. Always this stream is a great deal bigger water than the Exe is at Exford, yet it resorteth into Exe river. . . . From Simonsbath bridge I rode up a high moorish hill and so passing by two miles in like ground, the soil began to be somewhat fruitful and the hills to be full of enclosures until I came a three miles farther to a poor village called Brayford, where runneth a brook. . . .'

The old chap's miles were certainly long ones!

HUNTING RIGHTS

The sixteenth century also saw the beginnings of modern stag-hunting. The sport that we know today, with the practice of keeping a resident pack of staghounds upon the moor, may be said to have its beginnings with the year 1508, when the Crown for the first time granted a lease of the forest, together with the full hunting rights, to a private person. Hitherto the wardens of the forest had no hunting rights other than such as might be occasionally granted to them by special licence, but henceforth the lessee-warden or his deputy might keep hounds and regard the deer as his own property. This first lessee was Sir Edmund Carew, a knight of Devonshire, and the grant gave him the specific right to 'hunt and course the deer, stags as well as bucks and does . . . with hounds, greyhounds . . . but so nevertheless that on the day of his death the said Edmund he leave a hundred deer, stags and bucks and does in the said Forest or Chase of Exmoor. . . .' Were there really fallow deer on Exmoor at that time? Probably the phrasing is purely rhetorical.

The first definite statement about hounds and hunting on Exmoor is that which affirms that Sir Hugh Pollard, ranger and warden of the forest in the latter part of the reign of Queen Elizabeth, kept staghounds at Simonsbath. That he maintained a pack of staghounds is likely enough, but he could not have kept them at Simonsbath, for there was no dwelling there before Boevey's house of 1653. Sir Hugh himself abode at King's Nympton, so perhaps the hounds were kennelled there too.

PETTY QUARRELS

For the rest, the records of the sixteenth and early seventeenth centuries are but of personal disputes, lawsuits and various petty claims and offences. There is all the usual tale of quarrels and infringements that one might expect—of quarrels between the forester and the Free Suitors concerning rights and duties, of certain Free Suitors turning out upon the forest beasts not their own, of unringed pigs being turned upon the forest with disastrous effect upon the pasture, of a certain suitor keeping a 'fowling-piece and a crossbow' and swearing that he did so 'for the defence of his own house and not otherwise', of fishing with unlawful nets, and of poaching salmon by night, as on the occasion when Thomas Williams of Withypool and some others were caught taking fish with salmon-spears, by the light of a fire-torch, out of the Barle between Landacre Bridge and Oxen Pool.

With regard to pigs, they had long been looked upon with disfavour in the forest, as they were said to drive the deer away, and had even been accused of killing sheep and lambs, and in a deposition of 1608 the following remarkable happening is recorded:

'About 40 years now last past, this deponent's father,

having turned certain pigs into the said forest, did for two years miss one of his pigs, during which time many complained that they had sheep killed in the said forest, but by what means they could not tell; at length in the time of a snow the track or footsteps of a swine were espied, which was followed to a certain cave or hole in the said forest, where they found the said swine, and thereupon it was generally supposed that the said swine had killed many sheep in the said forest. . . .'

Shades of the wild boar! Had the creature really killed and eaten mutton for a livelihood? (Quite likely, for farmyard sows of today have been known to snap up wandering lambs.) Could such an animal really be considered as domestic? Very likely these old pigs of the hill country had a strong strain of the now extinct wild boar stock in them, even as the Tamworth is said to have in its ancestry. Anyway, subsequent to this pigs seem to have been generally debarred from the forest.

A frequent cause of trouble was the straying into the forest of stock pastured on the local commons. As there was no hedge or visible boundary of any sort to prevent this, the happening was more or less continuous and could be held in check only by constant vigilance and herding. Concerning this there could be unscrupulousness on both sides. A notable case was that of John Slowley of Eastcott and John Pearse, forester. This tale has been told often enough, but is worth telling again, as it shows well how things went on in those days and times.

It appears that Slowley had a large flock of sheep upon Porlock common, and that they, or some of them, were in the habit of straying into the forest. The forester demanded payment for their continued trespass, but Slowley refused. Thereupon Pearse ordered his men to seize the said sheep, which they set out to do, but on coming to the place upon the forest where the sheep were wont to be, found them gone out to the common again. Angry at being balked, the men determined to fake the evidence. Two of them rode out to the common and drove some forty-five of Slowley's sheep over the bounds into the forest, whereupon the other two hands, who had waited at Black-barrow, took possession of the sheep and then altogether the nefarious party rode triumphantly back to Withypool. Unfortunately for them, one Andrew Stone of Culbone, who had gone out to look for some cattle, saw all these proceedings from an unobserved position. Meanwhile, on being informed that his sheep had been impounded, Slowley sent his nephew to Withypool to treat with Pearse, but apparently nephew and forester got to loggerheads, and young Slowley came home empty-handed. By that time Slowley senior seems to have had word with Andrew Stone, and the next journey upon which the nephew was sent was to Willeton for a writ for the recovery of his sheep. But the writ was treated with contempt by the forester, who declared the sheep forfeit and had them taken to his own place at North Molton. After this there followed a court case, in which Slowley came off best, the forester being ordered to restore or pay the full value of the sheep plus damage. Such is a fair example of life and scandal upon Exmoor in the year 1622.

The round of life goes on, with squabbles about this and that, and louder grumbles at the gradual rise in the prices for agistment (inflation being no new thing). Then, in 1633, the question of tithes raised its ugly head. Hitherto, Exmoor Forest being extraparochial, the farmers by agisting their stock had escaped the payment of tithes upon these animals. Now claim and demand for tithes upon such beasts was made from various quarters. What may be called a 'tithe war' followed, which ensued with much litigation for some twenty years. First the clergy claimed tithes, then the Crown did so, with the ultimate result that after numerous court cases the man of Exmoor had to accept defeat and pay tithe on their depastured animals to someone or other. This was a severe blow to the hill farmers, and as a result the numbers of sheep summered on the Forest is said to have dropped from 20,000 to 14,000.

THE CIVIL WAR

The Civil War, which broke out in 1642, did not greatly affect Exmoor (though there were a few affrays in the neighbouring townships), but on several occasions troops of cavalry, both Royalist and Parliamentarian, passed over the high moors *en route* for more important places.

In 1642 some of Hertford's Cavaliers passed through Exford. In 1644 more Royalists, under Sir Francis Dodington, went from Minehead to Ilfracombe across Exmoor, and later in the same year a large body of Parliamentary cavalry, withdrawing from Barnstaple, crossed Exmoor on their way to Taunton.

It was in 1645, though, that Exmoor saw a nobler and more brilliant cavalcade: in June of that year Prince Charles (later Charles II), set out from Dunster Castle to ride to Barnstaple, where he hoped to find a safe refuge both from his opponents and from the plague which was then rife in parts of Somerset. The prince was accompanied by the Bishop of Salisbury, Lord Capel, Lord Colepeper, Sir Edward Hyde, the Earl of Brentford (Lord Ruthven) and Mr Richard Fanshawe; also three ladies, Mrs Fanshawe, Lady Capel and Lady Brentford, and the company was escorted by three troops of Lord Hopton's horse under Lord Hopton himself. Prince Charles was at that time about fifteen years old. Surely the sun must have shone on that brilliant scene! The cantering horses, the tossing plumes, the rich uniforms, the flash and jingle of bits and spurs and scabbarded swords—so for the span of a few hours a royal prince came again to ancient Exmoor.

LEASE OF THE FOREST

On the Parliamentary party being victorious, however, steps were taken for the survey and sale of the Crown land of Exmoor Forest. The survey took place in 1651, and the published statement contains much that is of interest. The bounds arc given thus: 'Ridge Stone' (Redstone?), 'Homlymeade

Post' (Honeymead Cross?), 'Ridgehill', 'Champards Ball', to the River Barle, 'Kingsborne Pitte' (Kinglands Pits), 'Dillacombe', 'Weston Hascome' (Halscombe), 'Middle Hascombe', 'Litten Ball' and 'Litten Foote', 'Litten Brooke' to a 'highway' from Withypool to Molland (Sandy Way?), 'Coles Cross', 'Buttery Corner', 'Shirkham Ridge', 'Redway', 'Five Barrowes', 'Settaborrowe', 'Kinisford Ball' and 'Kinisford Barrowe', 'Moles Chamber', 'Challacombe Ball', 'Longstone', 'Loughton Ball', 'Woodberrowe Hill' and 'Woodberrowe', 'Sadley Stone Ball', and 'Sadley Stone' (Saddle Stone), 'Horeoak Ball' and 'Horeoak', 'Hore Tarr' and 'Hore Tarr Combe', 'to the head of Batchery Combe' and 'down by the Combe to the Batchery Inclosure' (Badgery or Badgeworthy), along the water to 'where it meets the Pinsford River', 'Mightye Combe', 'Sawforth Brooke', (Stowford Bottom), 'three comb in feet' (Three Combes Foot), 'Blaykborrowe Topp' (Blackbarrow), 'Owlamans Borrowe' (Alderman's Barrow), 'Larkborrowe Topp', 'Sprecham Brook', 'along by the ground called Orchard and Redbrookes House', down the Exe and up 'Exridge' and 'Kitteridge' 'unto the ridge stone'.

This perambulation shows Oare to have long since passed out of the forest. For the rest the bounds are almost identical with those of the third perambulation. At two points, though, they are not precisely clear: the 'Longstone' referred to must surely be the Edgerly Stone, and not the tall monolith a little to the west, which we know as the Longstone. Also, 'Batchery Combe' is confusing. One would suppose it to be Hoccombe Water, were it not for the mention of the enclosure at the foot—there has never been any trace or tradition of a holding here. But in the next, more northerly combe (the so-called Doone Valley), there has always been a settlement of sorts, and this would answer best to the description. As to the mention of 'Redbrookes House', there used to be an old farmstead in Orchard Bottom, but the ruins have now quite disappeared.

The condition and nature of the forest is further summed up
as:

> 'Mountainous and cold ground, much beclouded with
> thick fogs and mists and is used for agisting and depastur-
> ing of cattle, horses and sheep, and is very sound sheep
> pasture, but a very great part thereof is overgrown with
> heath, and yielding but a poor kind of turf of little value
> there, and a considerable part thereof lying upon the sides
> of the combes lies near the rock and is capable only of
> being a sheep pasture, and the residue thereof being only
> some of the balls or hills if they were enclosed might be
> capable of improvement being a good soil. . . .'

A very fair description, such as might pass today. One thing,
though, calls for comment, for it does not hold today: that is the
overgrowth of heath or heather. There is very little heather
within the area today, the herbage of the open forest consisting
almost entirely of moor-grass, sedge and rush. While there can
be no doubt that the wild heart of Exmoor has always been as it
still is, there is equally little doubt that there was in ancient
times far more heather upon those outer parts of the forest than
there is today. It seems to have been an offence to burn the
heath wantonly in olden times—probably because a thick mat
of heather and gorse was considered good cover for game—and
in 1640 we hear of one John Harton accused of burning an acre
or so of old overgrown heath in which his sheep had been
entangled, and his making answer that there were a thousand
acres more of such old heath within the forest, and that it would
be much better burnt. One must assume that in more recent
years the reclamation of much of the outer forest, with enclosure, frequent burning and probable liming, has checked or
destroyed the cover of heather.

JAMES BOEVEY

The forest, or 'chase', as it was now termed, was eventually
purchased by James Boevey of London, merchant. Boevey was

a remarkable man of Dutch extraction, having energy, vision and intellectual gifts, plus a desire for a country estate. Like many another nearer our own day, he had wearied of city life and its unhealthiness, and for the good of his body and soul had determined to embark upon the adventure of a country life. His first act, on his obtaining possession of the land in 1653, was to build himself a handsome house right in the centre of the ancient forest, and to establish a farm and some enclosures thereabouts. This, Simonsbath House, was and is a very fine place, long and dignified, well built of local stone, with big windows and fine panelling within, and far removed from the homely farmhouses of the surrounding parishes. Its erection was in its way an epoch-making event, for hitherto there had been no dwelling or buildings of any sort anywhere within the forest, and this new venture marked the beginning of a new era. Boevey seems to have made a good start, enclosing, manuring and generally improving the lands about his settlement (the Simonsbath enclosures totalled some 108 acres at the beginning of the nineteenth century, and this probably represents the extent of Boevey's original work), but soon—again like many a newcomer to a hill country—he 'got across' the local farmers and became engaged in a series of quarrels and arguments about their rights upon the moor. Not content with the extent of his own profit and authority over his own forest or chase portion of Exmoor, he then proceeded to carry the war into the enemy's camp by making some sort of claim to the surrounding commons, demanding tithes from their pasturage. According to his views, these areas of open moorland extending from the old hill-farm enclosures up to the bounds of the ancient forest were not truly part of the parishes they represented, but were in some sense an extension of the forest.

A bitter legal battle ensued. The commons in question, which completely encircled the central forest, were those of Oare, Porlock, Stoke Pero, Exford, Withypool, Hawkridge, Molland, Twitchen, North Molton, High Bray, Challacombe, Lynton,

Brendon and Badgeworthy. The parsons and farmers of these moorland parishes rallied together to fight for the independence of their common land, and for five years the struggle went on in the courts, until at length, in 1679, Boevey had to retire defeated.

With the Restoration of 1660, Exmoor Forest automatically reverted to the Crown. James Boevey, however, though losing his freehold, was allowed to remain at Simonsbath as tenant until the time of his death. (He seems to have been astute enough to have bought out the Crown leases from their original holders, and so retained some legal right to the forest for his lifetime.) This latter part of his life seems to have been devoted mainly to further lawsuits with his neighbours. At length, in January 1696, he departed this life, having held Exmoor for forty-odd years.

James Boevey stands in the annals of Exmoor Forest a strange and disturbing figure. He had the gifts of intellect, vision, industry and ambition, yet he never went very far in life. His health, never very good, may have been one reason. His cantankerous nature was probably a greater reason. Could he have refrained from continuous quarrels with his neighbours, and from engaging in profitless litigation, he might have gone far indeed. The venture of buying the forest and building a house in its desolate heart was a valiant one, preceding the foresight of the Knights by nearly two hundred years. In him some flare of Jacobean land-pioneering or hardy Dutch enterprise must still have burned. Perhaps the moor drew him as it has drawn so many. One wonders how he liked living at Simonsbath, and if he was there often. The house, fine though it was, must have been very lonely, especially in the winter, for the nearest neighbour was Landacre, away down the Barle many miles off, and there were no roads save the roughest of moorland tracks. In his later life he had antagonized every farmer and parson on Exmoor, so he could have had little hope of the neighbourliness that is the essence of hill-country life, and would have no friendly visitors to the place. Of his dreams and projects, if he had any, nothing remains, but Simonsbath House still stands and is his memorial.

THE LEGEND OF THE DOONES

Before leaving the seventeenth century, something should possibly be said about the 'legend of the Doones', for it is in the latter part of this period that the tale is usually set. Blackmore, in his famous romance *Lorna Doone*, makes the Doones to be a gang of outlaws living in Badgery Water, and their leader a nobleman of Scottish extraction. He—Blackmore—probably based his story on tales that were current around Exmoor and north Devon in his time, but to what extent he invented both the characters and events of his book cannot now be said. Possibly it is wholly a romance. Certainly his description of the 'Doone Valley' is so, for though each of the natural features quoted may be found somewhere or other on Exmoor, they nowhere occur together, and not at all in Badgery.

It is a good tale, though, and gives a vivid picture of life as it must often have been in a wild country in the days when no proper enforcement of law was possible. That bands of lawless men, deserters from armies, or fugitives from justice, should from time to time take up residence in some lonely part of the moor or in the deep woods, and for a while harry the country-side and defy all authority, is quite credible.

4. OF HUNTING AND FARMING

No spectacular events mark the eighteenth century upon Exmoor. A few travellers came and went, and passed comment on the country. Daniel Defoe came this way in 1724, *en route* from Barnstaple to Taunton, while engaged in his *Tour through the Whole Island of Great Britain*. What little he saw of Exmoor he did not like. Having taken a look at the northern sea coast, he then says: 'Leaving the coast we came, in our going southward, to the great river Ex, or Isca, which rises in the hills on this north side of the county . . . the country it rises in, is called Exmore, Cambden calls it a filthy, barren ground, and, indeed, so it is; but as soon as the Ex comes off from the moors and hilly country, and descends into the lower grounds, we found the alteration; for then we saw Devonshire in its other countenance, viz. cultivated, populous, and fruitful. . . .' This latter evidently appealed to him far more than the windswept heights.

The story of Exmoor during this period is almost entirely one of hunting, farming and some noteworthy landlords.

The eighteenth century is notable for the rise of the Acland family. This remarkable family, which originated in the fifteenth century, from Acland Barton in north Devon, had by a succession of successful marriages and other enterprises arisen by such time to be the greatest landowners upon and in the vicinity of Exmoor. At the height of their prosperity it was said of them that they might ride upon their own land all the way from Porlock Vale to Exeter. Pixton was theirs, and later Holnicote, and almost all the land on the eastern side of Exmoor right down to the family seat at Killerton.

A remarkable family they were indeed, men of great vigour, loving the open-air pursuits of hunting and farming, great landlords, masters of the staghounds and wardens of the forest, admired and respected by all.

NORTH DEVON STAGHOUNDS

It is with the Aclands that stag-hunting on Exmoor, as we know it today, really begins. As we have seen, throughout its history Exmoor had been a land devoted to hunting, but hitherto there had been no resident pack of hounds upon the moor (that is, unless we accept the statement that Hugh Pollard kennelled hounds at Simonsbath). Whosoever came to hunt upon Exmoor, princes, nobles or such gentlemen as had the right, brought their own hounds with them, and after their sport took their packs home again. Now, however, by the mid eighteenth century, we find a splendid pack of hounds, known as the North Devon Staghounds, in the possession of the Acland family and maintained by them for the purpose of hunting the wild red deer of Exmoor.

The curtain rises, as it were, somewhere about 1750 with this noble pack in the hands of Sir Thomas Dyke Acland (1st) at Pixton. From whence came these great hounds, so widely known and famed in the west down to the year 1825? According to a letter written by Lord Graves to Lord Ebrington in 1812, the first Sir Thomas had them from his kinsman, Mr Dyke of Holnicote, who himself had them from Lord Orford. Before this they were kept by the dukes of Bedford at Tavistock, from whence they hunted the wild red deer of Dartmoor—Dartmoor was at that time as great a red deer country and famed hunting-ground as Exmoor itself. There is another tradition that the hounds came from Mr Walter of Stevenstone, who hunted deer

SIR THOMAS ACLAND'S HOUNDS

in the country between Hatherleigh and Torrington during the early part of the eighteenth century, but this seems less likely than the former assumption.

(Incidentally the lease and wardenship of the Forest of Exmoor had passed in 1737 to the earls of Orford, and was held by them until 1774, from which year the lease went to the Aclands, who remained wardens until 1814. So it seems probable that Lord Orford's hounds were hunting on Exmoor during his lease.)

A noble pack they certainly were. Dr Collyns, who knew them well and hunted often with them in the days of his youth, has left us an eye-witness description of them. They were, he says, from twenty-six to twenty-eight inches in height, badger-

91

pied, or yellow and white in colour, deep in muzzle, throat and chest, and with long pendulous ears. (Some while ago I was shown a contemporary painting of two of these hounds, and the impression given was of creatures tremendously powerful, looking more like something between a bloodhound and a mastiff than a hound of today.) Their great cry was wonderful, and could be heard from an immense distance. For nose and persistence, and the working out of a difficult line, especially along the water, they were without equal. If their pace was slow according to modern standards, it was amply made up for by their unswerving endurance, hunts of tremendous length— fifty miles or more as hounds ran—being recorded. Yet they cannot have been so very slow, judging by some of the runs that have been chronicled, and Collyns himself says that few horses could live with them in the open.

VARIOUS MASTERS

Sir Thomas Acland kept the hounds until 1775, then Colonel Basset of Watermouth Castle took them for ten years, from 1775 to 1785. They returned to the Aclands in 1785, and Sir Thomas Dyke Acland (2nd) kept them until 1794.

Those were the great days of staghunting. Into the hands of the second Sir Thomas—known as 'His Honour'—had come, by inheritance, Highercombe and Pixton and Holnicote, and in the south Killerton and most of the lands between, so that it was said he could ride from Holnicote to Killerton, near Exeter, all the thirty miles of the way upon his own land. He maintained the hounds and the dignity of the mastership, as he did everything else, in princely style. The pack was kennelled at Highercombe, while Sir Thomas resided at Pixton and there kept open house on hunting days. At the early morning meets there might assemble five hundred horsemen, and in the evening, when the chase was done, all who were at the finish were bidden to dinner with the master. And how famed was the hospitality of Pixton in those days! How honoured and respected the name of Sir Thomas both as sportsman and landowner!

On the death of Sir Thomas in 1794, Colonel Basset again had the hounds and kept them until 1801. Then in 1802 they went to Castle Hill, where the first Earl Fortescue hunted them for a season. After that a Mr Worth of Worth House, Tiverton, took over the management, and kept them as a subscription pack until the year 1810. Then Lord Graves had them for one season and then, in 1812, he made them over to Lord Fortescue.

With the coming of the hounds again to Castle Hill, there began a second great period of staghunting upon Exmoor. For the next six years, until 1818, the sport shown by the Fortescues, and the hospitality shown by Castle Hill, worthily rivalled that of the Aclands of Pixton. Again there were long days of sport on the high moor, and evenings of feasting and drinking to finish those days, and all was well with the country.

In 1818 Mr Lucas of Baronsdown assumed the mastership, and kept the pack until 1825, when the old order of things finally came to an end.

HUNTING DIARIES AND RECORDS

As to the sport itself, the records show it to have been the best possible, conducted in a manner that has not changed to this day, and the customs of which—such as harbouring, tufting and laying-on the pack—very probably had come down unaltered from very ancient times. The only difference between then and now was that the meets were held very early and tufting started at nine o'clock—Lord Graves seems to have considered that late in the day, and advocates eight o'clock at the latest—and that the practice of spring staghunting had not then come into fashion. Runs were often very long (it must be remembered that the whole of high Exmoor was then unenclosed), and times and distances great.

The earliest detailed record that we have of a run with these famous hounds comes from a letter, written in September 1759, by one J. Rich, park keeper to Courtenay Walrond, Esq., to an Exeter friend. According to this missive, a great run was had the preceding week, a stag being roused at the head of Iron Mill Water and running to Stuckeridge Wood, over the Exe, on to Exe Cleeve, right over Exmoor Forest, to be finally killed at Lowry Gate, 'the whole more than seventy miles' (which is probably an exaggeration, even as hounds ran). The stag had all his rights, and seven on one top and five on the other, and was to one inch fourteen hands high 'and appeared to be about ten years old'. The writer notes that there were at the chase more than five hundred horses and '1,000 foot'—that is to say, at the meet, which is not named—and at the end of the run there were some twenty gentlemen up, who returned to Pixton with Sir Thomas and there 'drank the health of the stag in a full quart of claret placed in the stag's mouth', and then next day dined with Sir Thomas 'on a haunch of this noble creature and about fifty dishes of the greatest rarities, amongst which were, with several other, black grouse'. What sport and what feasting indeed!

The two main chronicles of the sport of these great days of the old North Devon Staghounds are, firstly, the hunting diary of John Boyce, sporting parson of Withypool, in which are noted most of the runs from 1776 to 1816 and, secondly, the journal kept by the Fortescue family for the years 1812–18. To these may be added Collyns's own diary kept from 1816 to 1824. These together give many vivid pictures of long hard-riding days on the high moor and in the deep wood-choked valleys, in times when there was no metalled road from end to end of the country, nor any strand of wire, nor any sound of machinery, and only the pounding of a horse's hooves to carry a man with the flying, crying hounds over the open ground. One thing, though, should I think be taken with caution: this is the mileage distance of the runs, especially as given by Boyse. Such maps as existed in those days were probably not very accurate, and any man's mental assessment of a mile was more or less arbitrary. On checking given names and points against a modern ordnance map, I find almost all distances considerably overestimated. I do not think the old chroniclers deliberately exaggerated, but, as I said, they were not always right in their reckoning.

Even after correcting the distances as given, some very great runs indeed are recorded with the old North Devon Staghounds. Points of up to twenty miles are not infrequent, with the distance as hounds ran being often quite double that length.

How these old entries make the days come alive again! (*see* Appendix D). How all the place-names, unchanged still, ring and echo in one's heart, and how in one's dreams one hears again the sound of a distant horn and the far-off baying of the great hounds!

Alas, nothing endures for ever, and this noblest of all packs hunted its last season in 1825. In that year it was sold, the buyer being a German baron, and the great cry of the old North Devon Staghounds was heard no more on the moor. Why was so famous a pack sold? No one seems to know for certain, and those chroniclers living nearer to the event seem not to have been very keen to go into details. The nearest one can get to any sort of truth is to say that the Mr Lucas who was the last master seems to have got into difficulties with the country, financial and otherwise. It would appear that subscribers and supporters were not satisfied with the way he was hunting the country, and so stopped paying their subscriptions, with the inevitable results. One wonders what happened to these great hounds. They are said to have been taken to Germany to hunt deer and wild boar in the Teutonic forests. For how long did they retain their identity, and do any known descendants exist today? One would like to know, but there seems no answer.

Incidentally it must in all truth be confessed that these splendid hounds had one grave fault which may have contributed to the embarrassment of their last master: they were inclined to sheep-killing. In the edited and printed extracts of the old hunting diaries such lapses from virtue are not mentioned, but in the originals they do appear. As in Parson Boyce's fine old diary, the faded brown handwriting not infrequently records, 'hounds also killed sheep'. Such laconic comments suggest a good deal more than they actually tell.

THE QUARTLYS OF MOLLAND

During the eighteenth century the hill farming of Exmoor, though continuing mainly in the traditional, immemorial fashion of the country, was much influenced by the big landowning families of the region—notably the Aclands—and in particular by a remarkable farming family called Quartly.

The Quartlys settled at Molland some time about the beginning of the eighteenth century, leasing, it seems, the whole parish from Lord Courteney. Two brothers, Henry and James, came to reside at the two manor farms—West Molland Barton and Molland Chamson or Great Chamson—and from thence began to farm their lands with ideas far in advance of their time. They and their families prospered, and the neighbouring farmers were much impressed and sought to copy their methods as far as they were able.

They—the Quartlys—had some knowledge of engineering, and one of their innovations was to cut many miles of guttering on their lands to bring the fresh moorland water to their fields for the irrigation of their grass and crops, and by this means amazing growth was produced. So successful was this method of watering that all over the hill country enterprising farmers adopted the practice, with the result that to this day one may trace upon many an Exmoor hillside the sunken rush-filled gutter lines that once carried the refreshing water from the spring-head to the sunny slopes. (I myself know of at least two farms where this method of watering is still in use; the water flows along the horizontal channel about the curve of the hillside, and each day the edge of the guttering is breached at different intervals to allow the water to spill over and run down the slope. By this alternate breaching and stopping, the whole hillside may be evenly irrigated, so producing a wonderful flush of spring grass.)

The achievement, however, for which the Quartlys are most famed and remembered is the improvement and final perfecting of the famous Devon cattle. The red Devon cattle, as has already been noted, would seem to be indigenous, had been recognized and remarked upon in Elizabethan times, and were already well known in the eighteenth century for their good qualities as draught oxen and as producers of beef and milk. The Quartlys devoted themselves to acquiring the best strains of this remarkable western breed that they could get, and from them bred cattle of a sort that were outstanding, both for work and beef. To the Quartlys, together with one or two other dedicated breeders such as the Davys of Rose Ash, we owe the Devon as we know it today.

From John Billingsley's book, *Agriculture of the County of Somerset*, compiled in 1795, and from the writings, etc., of various other persons, we can draw a fair picture of the farming on and about Exmoor during the eighteenth and early nineteenth centuries.

THE FIRST ORDNANCE SURVEY MAP

One of the most interesting documents of the time is the first ordnance survey map of 1809, for this shows us the land as it was then, and prior to the extensive enclosure that followed soon after. Here we see a huge expanse of moorland, extending, in an unbroken sweep of bent, fern and heather, unbounded by any wall, from Porlock to Bratton Fleming, from the sea coast to Molland and Anstey. In the midst of the area is the Royal Forest and about it are the commons of all the adjacent parishes. All around, the hill farms stand like islands in the waste. Roads in the proper sense there are none, only lanes between the fields and tracks across the moor. To what degree this first map is accurate in minor details is a matter of doubt—hill-country surveying was probably not very specific then—but enough is conveyed to give the substance of land and scenery of the time.

HILL FARMS OF THE EIGHTEENTH CENTURY

Of the actual farms and their buildings, Billingsley and his fellows have little to say, except that by counselling the erection of more farm buildings they imply a lack, and consider the hill farms small. Some rebuilding there was, though, for a number of our farmhouses show signs of eighteenth-century improvement, and one at least was completely rebuilt: the house at Landacre, which dates from the year 1760, and is a good example of a Georgian farmhouse, being plain and substantial, with lofty, well-proportioned rooms.

The fields of the time were small and irregular and mostly of only a few acres extent. They were bounded by high earthen banks, six or seven feet high, faced often with stone—the immemorial 'dyking' or 'ditching' of the moor—and topped with beech hedge. At least this last was the practice on the south-east side of Exmoor, for Billingsley praises the fine beech hedges upon the banks around Dulverton and Dunster, saying how well they withstood the wild wind from the sea, and commenting on the considerable amount of wood which they gave when laid. He mentions also the method of planting: three rows of young saplings about one foot apart, the middle row to be cut to the ground at maturity, while the outside ones are plashed. On the higher and more westerly parts of Exmoor, though, the banks were not planted with beech until after the Knights had introduced the practice on their newly reclaimed forest land—around Exford and Withypool the banks were topped only by gorse and scrub until within the past hundred years. (I have often heard a farmer friend speak of this, saying how his grandfather remembered it.)

The small fields were devoted partly to arable and partly to grass. Oats, wheat, beans, pease, vetches and turnips are mentioned. Oats were the principal corn crop, though one gathers that enough wheat was grown—of necessity—for the provision of bread. As to the method of cropping and rotation, there seems to have been several sorts, ranging from bad to good. The worst was that of simply taking up a piece of old pasture, sowing it with corn, taking off what crop one could get from it and then letting the ground lie fallow to recover how it could. A more general system was that of sowing first oats, then, after manuring, wheat, then turnips, then oats again, and after that putting down to grass for several years. Some time during the early part of the nineteenth century a new and better system was adopted: turnips or rape, then oats or wheat, then swedes, then down to grass again for several years. This last rotation is the one that has endured to the present day and is still practised on those farms which grow a little corn for their own use.

As to grass, Billingsley notes that the hill country naturally produces 'a variety of excellent sorts of grass', but mentions also that 'artificial grasses' are sown, and specifies broad and white clover, trefoil and 'ray-grass called here evergrass' (rye grass?). He counsels that any low-lying rich meadow should not be ploughed.

The watering of hillsides is also noted, and the remarkable results therefrom. By this means a farmer may have grass 'fit to receive ewes and lambs as early as Candlemass', and to carry the flock into May when, the land being unstocked and watered again 'after six or seven weeks, they mow from thirty cwt. to forty cwt. per acre' of hay from these slopes.

Manures consisted mainly of farmyard dung and ash, and to this Billingsley recommends the addition of crushed bone and hoof-parings, pond sludge, old woollen rags and as much lime and chalk as possible. For arable, he says the quantity of manure should not be less than 'one hundred and twenty horse-seams' of dung, or fifteen hogsheads of lime. The 'horse-seam' was the pack-horse load, and the 120 equivalent to twelve cartloads. With regard to the ash, this was the rich peat and wood ash from the hearth fire, carefully saved through the long winter. Most farms had their ash-house, which was a little building with a door on one side and a small aperture, low down on the ground, closed with a shutter on the other. In this place the ash was stored until the spring, when it was drawn out through the small opening and taken to dress the early grass. (Knowing something of the wonderful effect of wood-ash upon growing things, I can readily imagine its benefits to the little grass fields of Exmoor.)

OX TEAMS

The cattle of the hills were the red Devons. Here on the hill farms they were bred and raised, spending their first summers upon the moorland or the commons, or on the high forest, and their winters in the little fields or the dim shippons. Fine beasts they were, and here in the area between Porlock and Barnstaple they were at their best and purest. Two purposes they had in life: draught and beef, and to these might be added the desirable propensity to milk well. For the two first missions in life they had to maintain a balance of form that rendered them strong-boned enough for the plough, yet not too coarse for fattening.

For work at the plough they were unrivalled. They would exert their strength to the utmost, sustaining where necessary a dead-pull which very few horses could or would attempt. Yet they were agile, and moved freely and, in those parts where carts were in use, they would trot with an empty wagon at the rate of six miles to the hour, which was an accomplishment unknown to any other breed of cattle. Four oxen would do the work of any three horses, and with a double-furrow plough might plough as much as two acres of arable in one day. They were docile and good tempered, and honest in all their work.

Young steers were first yoked to the plough at three years old. They were introduced to the work in the company of older oxen and thereafter worked until they were about six years old. They were yoked in pairs—they were not worked in collars— and four oxen, full grown, made the standard team, though if young bullocks were used the team might consist of six beasts. (The old eight-ox team seems to have passed away with the Middle Ages.) A man and a boy were necessary to each team— the man to drive the plough and the boy to guide the leading oxen, and both sang at their work. The general conformation of the Devon working ox was one adapted to both strength and agility: the head was fine, with long slender horns, the forehand very powerful and rising high, the withers fine, the shoulders sloping, the breast broad and deep, the forelegs wide apart 'like pillars that have to support a great weight', and straight with powerful forearm, the back straight, the hindquarters long and full, and the tail set on high. The feet were seldom shod, as they were exceptionally strong and healthy. The skin, despite the curling hair, was fine and thin, and the colour of the coat a rich deep red. All who saw these beasts praised them.

At the age of about six years, when he was deemed full grown, the ox was taken from the plough and fattened for beef. This he did quickly, in the space of less than a year, for ability to fatten was one of the noted Devon attributes. If summer grass was good he required no other food, though if over-wintered he needed good finishing on hay, corn and turnips. The meat was of first-class quality. As to the practice of working before fattening, this was considered necessary, apart from economic use, in order to develop fully the frame of the beast for the subsequent carrying of flesh. Our present-day ideas of eating only youthful meat are very modern indeed, and had no place in our ancestors' times.

SHEEP

Sheep then, as now, were the prevailing stock of the hill farms. The horned Exmoors were the native breed and comprised the flocks of the higher and more remote farms, but another improved sort was known and bred about the moor; these latter were polled, and known as the Nott sheep.

The native Exmoors were little thought of by progressive

agriculturists. They were horned and goat-like, and kept for their shear of wool—about four pounds—rather than for mutton. However, they cost little in the way of keep, being mostly run on the hill, and thus fitted into the primitive economy of the moor. The ewes came in-ground during the winter and for the spring lambing, but the wethers were turned away on the hill all the year, coming down only for the shearing. These wethers were kept as wool sheep until they were about five years old, then they were brought down to the farm, fed on turnips and sold for what they would fetch. Some, however, were sold as hoggets after fattening on turnips, for Billingsley mentions such in South Molton market, and says their carcass weight was from 14 to 18 lb. per quarter. (This is a high estimate, for another writer says they seldom exceed 12 lb. a quarter.) The breed might be improved, but it was generally found, as is the case with most moorland creatures, that the improvement reduced the extreme hardiness necessary for survival on the hills. The name 'Porlock sheep' was sometimes applied to the Exmoor.

The second sort, the Devon Nott sheep, sometimes called the Bampton, was a more valued breed, and kept where better grass was available. These sheep were hornless and carried long thick fleece, and were described as being 'not much unlike the Leicester'. The wool clip was about 7 lb. Wethers were fattened and sold as two-tooths, and might reach carcass weight of 24 lb. a quarter. In many ways these sheep seem to have been the forerunners of the Closewool.

Of pigs there is little mention. The large herds of swine of the early Middle Ages had long disappeared, and one may suppose that the unnoticed cottage pig of the time was a nondescript animal, probably long-legged, and of consequence only to its owner.

EXMOOR PONIES

Creatures of the moor of much importance to the hill farms were the ponies. These almost wild, incredibly hardy little horses, who lived out their lives on moor and forest, were of value not only as small general purpose animals but also as foundation stock for the breeding of bigger sorts, either pack-horse or hunter. Most farmers would keep a small herd on the hill, one would guess, even as they do today (or did—not many ponies are on the hill now), whilst upon the forest a large number were maintained by the warden. Billingsley, when passing over Exmoor Forest, saw this herd of ponies and commented upon them: 'The small horses (in the whole upwards of four hundred) are not taken into better keeping nor to more sheltered grounds, during the severest winter. When the snow covers the forest to the depth of many feet these hardy animals are seen in droves traversing the little valleys and sheltered parts, gathering their scanty fare from the banks of rivulets and warm springs. . . .' Annual sales were held at Simonsbath for the disposal of the young stock from this herd, and buyers came from far and wide. The old account books of the forest give many interesting details. In size and appearance the ponies of the time cannot, in general, have differed from those of today—the true moorland type is unchanging, the form being governed by natural conditions and by the rigours of natural selection—but one or two mentions of 'grey' and 'chestnut' strike an odd note, until one remembers that there was, until comparatively recently, both a grey and a chestnut strain in the famous Acland herd, deriving from the forest ponies. It is significant that both these strains died out, which would seem to indicate that they were originally induced by crossing, and were consequently less hardy than the brown, bay and dun which are the accepted natural colours.

PACK-HORSES

Of all the animals on the hill farm, though, it was the pack-horses that were the most important, for upon them depended all transport and all work save the ploughing. For Exmoor was still pack-horse country. There were no roads, only muddy tracks and narrow stony lanes, and no wheeled vehicle had ever found its way into the hills. (It was not until the 1830's that the first carts made their appearance.) Everything went by pack-horse—hay to the rick, corn to the barn, manure out to the field, peat down from the hill, produce to market and merchandise from township to village. Even chimney-pots: in 1817 the Rector of Selworthy ordered some new chimney-pots for his rectory from Barnstaple, and they came all the way by pack-horse. The invoice reads: 'For six chimney Tops, £1 10s. 0d. Carriage for same from Barnstaple on three horses, 25 miles by Exmoor, 15s.'

A document from Molland, drawn up during the Napoleonic Wars, takes a census of all the working horses in the parish. It gives the total number as eighty-seven, of which eighty were pack-horses, and only seven cart-horses. So even in the country on the edge of the moor, carts had hardly made their appearance by the beginning of the nineteenth century.

As to this essential beast of burden, what manner of horse was he? Throughout the west the Devonshire pack-horse was a well-known creature, but for most parts was, like the hunter, a type rather than a breed. In north Devon, however, and in the Exmoor country, the pack-horse was an animal of definite breeding. Snell, in his *Book of Exmoor*, says of him, 'He was bred by a packhorse from a packmare, and in some sort might be termed a thoroughbred. Generally about 15 hands high, it was impossible to conceive a more useful animal. . . .' He was said also to be surefooted, good-looking, with a good shoulder, and to be a good trotter. Tradition credited the origin of this exceptional breed to a cross between a fine horse escaped from a Spanish wreck—a common fable—and the small native mares. Whatever the cross-breeding may have been, certainly the native Exmoor pony was the root and foundation of the stock, and it was to this blood that the pack-horse owed its strength, hardiness and surefootedness.

For work on the farm the pack-horse had two sorts of tackle

PACK-PONIES BRINGING IN THE HARVEST

or harness: the panniers and the crooks. The panniers were used for the transport of dung, peat or any other loose commodity. They seem to have been made with a trap-door bottom, so that when carrying manure, and the place of deposit having been reached, the pins were drawn out and the load dropped to the ground in two small heaps. The crooks were for the carrying of hay, sheaves and faggots, or any other bulky stuff. They were big yoke-like frames, usually made of willow, set upon the pack-saddles, and on them the loads were laid lengthwise and roped down.

Celia Fiennes, riding back in September 1698 from her tour of Cornwall, saw the western harvest coming in on pack-horses. She gives a vivid eye-witness description of how the horses were loaded from head to tail, and so high that the loads were in danger of overbalancing, and how two persons had to walk with each load, one on each side, to try to support and balance it while the horse picked its way over rough ground. At a much later date one hears an account from the Brendons of the haymaking, some time about 1830, with the hay coming up in like fashion. Here the horses were trained to come to the rick of their own accord, and on being unloaded they trotted back to the field again, so keeping up a ceaseless round.

For general transport the pack-horses went nine in a string, nose to tail, with bells upon the harness and the best horse in the lead. The average weight a horse might be expected to carry was about 240 lb., but some might take a load of as much as 400 lb. For long in the west the horse-load or 'seam' was a standard measure for farm stuffs, from wool to manure. (Note Billingsley's reference to the 'horse-seam'.)

COMMON RIGHTS

Throughout history, and until very recently, the economy of the hill farms depended greatly upon the moor and the common rights. All around the little enclosures lay the great wide wastes of heather and bent, wastes in name only, for they provided the hill farmer with a summer grazing for sheep and cattle, all-the-year-round grazing for ponies, peat for fuel, rushes for thatching and fern for bedding. The moor was a great reserve which gave much and cost nothing.

Every moorland parish or manor had its common—that is to say, the wastes of Exmoor outside the Royal Forest were divided up among these lordships—and all landholders within these bounds had their common rights.

Briefly, and in general, these rights were: the right to graze as many sheep, cattle and ponies as they could over-winter on their own farms (the ponies and the wether sheep, though, usually stayed out all the year), the right—called Turbary—to cut as much peat as they could burn on their own hearths, and the right to cut rush and fern for thatching and bedding. Without them the farms of Exmoor could hardly have existed.

THE FARMING YEAR

Let us take a look at the cycle of the farming year as it was then, had been from time immemorial and was still to be for a long while to come: through the dark days of winter the farmer and his beasts struggled towards the spring, always hoping for an early season and early grass (though all too often doomed to disappointment), eking out the dwindling hay and corn, and praying to be spared a late fall of snow. In March preparation would be made for lambing. April was the usual time for lambing in the hills, but even April can be a month of frost and snow on high ground, so good weather was doubly hoped for. Meanwhile the spring ploughing would be in hand, and the ground made ready for the corn. By May the grass should be growing, the leaves breaking on the beech hedges, and the summer ahead. The sheep would be restless in their small fields, and the cattle dissatisfied in the shippons. 'When the leaves are breaking on the beech it is time for the bullocks to go out,' it is said. Time to go out and up to the hill. Most of the flock went out to the common, and most of the cattle too. Those of the hill farmers who ranked as Free Suitors might drive their flocks and herds farther up into the forest, as they had the right to do. (Even if they had not the right, they might still find it worth their while to agist some of their stock on the forest.) This exodus of stock left most of the fields free to run for hay. By this time the 'muck' would have been drawn out of the yards and spread, the ground worked up and the spring corn planted (the beginning of May being the usual time for this). The last week in June all the sheep had to be gathered up and brought in for the great event of the year—the midsummer shearing. This was the great harvest of the moor, a time of hard work and a social gathering as well. Along with gruelling hard work there was feasting and fun, and dancing to finish with, and neighbours came together who might not see each other for the rest of the year. After the shearing the sheep went back to the hill. July was the month of haymaking (alas, all too often wet in the hills), when the grass was grown and folk struggled with the elements for that crop which spelt the difference between life and starvation for their beasts. In August the lambs were weaned, more hay battled for, crops hoed, weeds cut and innumerable other things attended to. On summer days when the weather was fine, and time could be spared away from the farm, the family would go up to the hill to cut peat from the bogs for the winter's fuel. (This turf would be dried and built up into small black ricks or 'turf-burrows'.) September was the harvest month, when the corn was reaped, and once again all hands battled with wind and rain for a precious crop. With plentiful hand labour, though, much could be done to save the grain which cannot be done today—the turning of sheaves, the making of windmows, and many another thing which no machine can do. A good harvest, in days of self-sufficiency, was indeed something to be thankful for. Now rush was cut from the moor for thatching the ricks, and also quantities of fern for winter bedding. At the end of October the beasts came down from the hills. All the cattle came in and most of the sheep, except the wethers, but the ponies stayed out to survive as they could. Briefly they were brought down to the yards for the annual 'drift', for the sorting and branding, but such stock as was not cut out for sale was at once turned back to the moor. Late summer and autumn was the season of sales and fairs, when the farmer reaped the reward of his labour and all surplus stock was got off the farm before the onset of winter. Then began all the winter tasks—the laying of hedges and the faggoting of brushwood, the threshing of corn in the barn with flails and the endless round of feeding the beasts. So the days shortened, with always the dread of a hard winter and the fear of the terrible blizzards that could cut off farm from farm for many weeks, perhaps months. After the cheer of Christmas, the deadness of January, then the turn of the year at Candlemas. 'Till Candlemas day keep half your hay.' It is a true saying, for in the hills it is February, not Christmastide, that marks midwinter, and one may have worse weather after than before. So it went on until the days lengthened and spring and its promise of life came to the land again.

As to the products that went off the hill farms, these were principally store cattle and sheep, young oxen for draught, some ponies and the annual wool clip. Such corn crops, or any other, as were grown were for home consumption only, but assorted farmhouse produce surplus to home needs would of course be taken down periodically to one or other of the small local markets. The commodities most likely to go jogging down the tracks and lanes in the ponies' panniers would be butter, cream, eggs (these latter would need careful packing!), poultry, pork and probably whortleberries in due season. Incidentally the name 'pannier market', applied to both Barnstaple and South Molton, perpetuates the memory of these days and ways.

The most immediate market townships providing a mart for the Exmoor farms would be Dunster and South Molton. Farther afield were Taunton and Wiveliscombe to the east, Tiverton to the south and Barnstaple, with its great Friday market, to the west.

In addition to the general weekly or monthly held markets there were, looming large in the hill-country calendar, the big annual or seasonal fairs.

The principal cattle fairs for the sale of the north Devon oxen were Ashbrittle, Bishop's Lydiard, Wellington, Barnstaple, Crediton, West Bagborough, Wiveliscombe, North Molton, Bampton and South Molton. These were all spring or early summer fairs, and are here given in order of date from February to June.

Bampton Fair, held the last Thursday in October, was always the principal horse and pony fair for the region.

One may guess at the great importance of such fairs and occasions in the lives of the hill folk, not only from the point of vital sales but also as journeyings to distant parts. What excitement! What glimpses of the wider world! One may be sure that pleasure was well combined with business on these big occasions.

As to the economic facts and figures, these are not easy to come by, and much must be guessed at. Farm leases and tenancies seem to have been of varying sorts, some long and some short. A common lease throughout Devon—indeed the most usual one—was the 'Lease of Three Lives', and most probably this prevailed upon Exmoor too. By this an incoming farmer nominated three lives for his tenure—usually himself, his wife and his eldest son—then paid a cash-down entry fine and thereafter a very small annual rent. It was a good lease, giving family security over a lengthy period, and should the farmer himself die his widow and children still had a home and a living. A classic example of the system is that of the Quartlys, who initially took Molland Champson under such a lease. The yearly value of the farm was assessed at £80, and they paid to the squire, John Courtenay, an entry fine of £778, and thereafter a nominal rent of £2 a year. By the beginning of the nineteenth century, however, ordinary rack-rents seem to have been usual for the lesser farms.

Exmoor farms were on the whole small ones, essentially family farms, worked by the holder and his wife and children. Hired labourers were the exception rather than the rule, except on the few big bartons. The lot of the labourer, where he existed, was a hard one, for in the West Country he might not receive more than seven shillings a week—a bare shilling a day—wherewith to bring up his often numerous family.

Stock prices fluctuated, much as they do today. On the

whole sheep seem to have been valued more for their wool than for their mutton. With regard to cattle, Billingsley refers to the Devon work oxen being sold off to graziers for prices ranging from £10 to £22. The Forest Book of 1736 (the earliest in existence) for entering of agisted stock of an Exmoor Forest gives the highest prices of 'colts' sold after a drift as £1 13s. 6d. for one and £3 9s. 6d. for two, with a lowest figure of 16s. for one.

The same account book gives the prices of agistment on the forest as: Sheep, commoners 2½d., others 3d. or 4d.; cattle, commoners 1s., strangers 2s.; horses, commoners 2s., strangers 4s. The Free Suitors, of course, paid nothing.

In addition to agriculture there was, upon the fringe of the moor, some woollen industry. North Molton flourished for a while on fulling and weaving, but this trade came to an end with the passing of the eighteenth century. In the latter parish there was also a certain amount of mining, mostly for iron or copper, though lead and some silver were also to be found.

This was the scene upon which Billingsley looked, and upon which he counselled the following improvements: the granting of long leases to give security and stability to the farmer, the provision of more buildings, the proper composting of manure, a liberal use of lime, a rotation of crops that would improve not deplete the soil, improvement of stock by selection or judicious crossing and a greater attention to grass. 'As in every point of view this country appears from its soil and situation to be better adapted to grass than arable, it deserves enquiry, whether stock could not profitably be kept on grass land alone. . . . Grass, therefore, should be considered as the ultimate improvement of land in the Western part of the county of Somerset.' In this he shows a true understanding of the nature of the country and a perception in advance of his time.

He also advises the improvement of roads and the planting of windbreaks to check the force of the western gales. Scots fir, beech, larch, sycamore, ash and birch are the trees most recommended.

As to the ancient forest, with the eighteenth century it enters into its last phase. Simonsbath House and farm now being in existence, and sited in the middle of the forest, the place became the residence of the deputy forester, and the general centre of administration for the business of the forest. Withypool and Hawkridge lost their old importance, and ceased to be the 'villages of the forest'.

FOREST ACCOUNTS

Billingsley remarks of it:

> 'Nearly at the centre of this large tract of land is an estate called Simonsbath, enclosed and consisting of about two hundred acres, with a dwelling house, licensed and frequented as an inn, and all offices belonging to it convenient for the management of the farm, and transacting the concerns of the forest. . . . On the summits of the hills especially on the West and North, are swamps of many acres extent. They are cut up as turf at the rate of eight-pence or twelve-pence per thousand paid to the tenant of the forest. . . . Excepting a few willows and thorns by the sides of the rivulets, not a tree or a bush out of Simonsbath estate is to be seen on the whole forest. . . .'

He notes that there are many springs and streams, giving an abundance of pure water. Also that the material for road-making lies all around. With regard to existent tracks he remarks that they are 'very bad, and in some places scarcely passable'.

He further remarks: 'A very large proportion of the whole needs but the spirit, and the fortune, of some one or more of our wealthy gentlemen in England, whose attention, if turned this way, sanctioned by the royal proprietor, would render the forest of Exmoor, in a few years, as fair a prospect as the surrounding country. . . .' Billingsley recommends enclosure, with the establishment of a village at Simonsbath, the planting of oak, pine, beech and elm plantations, and the reclamation of the land by paring and burning, 'the surface being burnt mixed with lime, would be a first dressing, preparatory to a crop of turnips or corn . . . the grain which thrives in the adjoining parishes would, no doubt, flourish here. . . .'

The old 'Forest Books', the old account books of this period, some of which have survived, give many interesting details of the agisting and general management of stock. The numbers of sheep depastured annually during the 1730's seems to have averaged some 37,400. Of these, 7,280 would come from the Free Suitors, the bordars or Suitors-at-Large sent about 14,000, and the remainder, some 16,000-odd, came from 'strangers'. Those parishes beyond the borders which sent flocks as strangers were Arlington, Ashford, Bishop's Nympton, West Buckland, East Buckland, Berrynarbour, Bishop's Tawton, Bickington, Bratton, Braunton, Bideford, Chittlehampton, Charles, East Down, Fremington, Goodleigh, Heanton, Kentisbury, Loxhore, Landkey, South Molton, Marwood, Filleigh, Swimbridge, Shirwell, Stoke Rivers, Tawstock, Warkley, West Down and Yearnscombe. The largest contingent, 2,915, came from Swimbridge; the smallest, thirty, from West Down, and the same also from Ashford. What a business it must have been sending the sheep up to the moor—and home again for shearing! In the case of a distant place like Bideford, the journey must have taken several days. And what a noise of sheep and barking of dogs and shouting of horsemen there must have been all about the moor as the wild-eyed flocks converged upon the forest heights, choking the narrow lanes as they came, or running wild on the intervening commons. The moor grazing must indeed have been deemed valuable for such migrations to be worth all the trouble and time. The rates for sheep per head at that time were $2\frac{1}{2}d.$ for borderers and $5d.$ for strangers.

Bullocks agisted at this time numbered only about 130 or less. Nearly all these came from the Somerset side and were the property of the local farmers. The rate was a shilling a head and two shillings for the few strangers who sent beasts. The horses numbered about a hundred, likewise nearly all from local folk. Their price was two shillings a head and four shillings for the few outsiders.

In addition to the agisted horses, though, there were others—the semi-wild Exmoor ponies of the forest. These were regarded as the property of the wardens, and were now managed from Simonsbath. No record of the actual numbers running on the forest is given, but there are entries for the periodic sale of colts, whose numbers vary from thirty-four to fifty at a time, which argues a fairly substantial herd of mares. (Billingsley says 'upwards of four hundred', and says that they never left the forest—*see* page 103.) Some attention seems to have been given to the breeding at this time, for there are entries for the occasional purchase of a new stallion, and for the sending down of the stallions to better pasture for the winter. The 'surveys' or sales seem to have been held at intervals of one or two years.

It would have been a happy thing if Exmoor Forest could have continued in the possession of the Aclands but, alas, the forest as such brought in very little revenue to the Crown, and by the end of the eighteenth century a move was made by Parliament to look into the financial aspect of this and other Crown lands. A survey of Exmoor Forest was undertaken and a report published in 1814.

This report gave among other things the following details: that the forest at its greatest extent measured about ten miles from north-west to south-east, and about seven miles from north-east to south-west. It contained approximately 22,000 acres of land, which were made up as follows: 8,050 acres, rushy land with sheep pasture; 5,190 acres, peat and moss land, swampy; 5,030 acres, ferny land with good sheep pasture; 2,040 acres, ferny land with thistles, excellent sheep pasture; 1,450 acres, heathy land with good sheep pasture; 240 acres, springy land (wet); 50 acres, furze land, good mould. The survey gives the soil as 'for the most part of a hazle loamy mould, frequently with a gravelly subsoil, that on the hills is black peaty earth, of good depth, but on a rocky bottom . . .', and notes that the valleys are 'deep ravines' giving little ground in their bottoms, but that there are wide plains upon the tops of the hills. Simonsbath Farm had enclosures totalling 108 acres, and the homestead had about it four ash trees, three large beech trees, twenty-three sycamores, and seven lime-pollards—thirty-seven in all, the only trees on the whole of the forest. The house itself was at that time licensed as an inn. The only industry, apart from the pasturing of beasts, was working of a slate quarry and some cutting of heath and turf for sale. The surveyors recommended the sale of the forest for enclosure.

DISAFFORESTATION

Sir Thomas Acland wished to purchase the freehold of Exmoor Forest, but it was not to be. In 1815 an Act for the disafforestation of Exmoor was passed, and commissioners were appointed to look into the rights of the moor folk, to make awards, fix boundaries and to mark highways. A last perambulation was made, and the ancient 'metes and bounds' of the old forest were by this last circuit set as follows: Hooked Stone, Halscombe, Litton Foot Stone, Willingford, Sandyway Stone, Coles Cross, Buttery Corner, Two Barrows, Horsehead Stone, Hore Stone or Sloley Stone, Settabarrow, Mole's Chamber, Long Stone, Edgerly Stone, Woodbarrow, Saddle Stone, Benjamy, Hoar Oak, Hoccombe, Longcombe, Longcombe Barrow, Tom's Hill Stone, Kittuck, Kittuck Barrows, Black Barrow, Owlaman's (Alderman's) Barrow, Lark Barrow, Spraccombe, Orchard Corner, Red Stone, Ashott Corner, Honeymead Corner, White Hill Stone, Sherdon Hutch, Sherdon Rock, Kingsland Pits, Dillacombe Hill and Landacre Hill. The days of the open forest were over. Its land was about to be dismembered and parcelled out.

The first awards were made in 1817. Sir Thomas Acland received, in lieu of the tithes of Exmoor, some 3,200 acres, considered to be equal in value to one-eighth of the forest. This allotment took up most of the land lying north of the Warren, and east of the Brendon road. The Free Suitors received allotments of thirty-one apiece—1,633 acres in all—from land abutting on to the Withypool and Hawkridge commons. On the surface this seems fair enough, but in actual fact it led to much bitterness and a feeling of injustice that lingered on for many years. The crux of the matter was that the awards were made to the landlords, not to the occupiers. One landlord, John Thornton, owned as many as seventeen of the Free Suitors' farms, and another, Lord Carnarvon, owned eleven. Such landowners indeed received substantial compensation, but the occupiers, the actual farmers to whom the grazing rights had meant so much, frequently received nothing. The landlords were themselves supposed to compensate their tenants, but it seems that in many cases they did not do so.

Lastly, awards were made to the Suitors-at-Large of the surrounding parishes in lieu of their loss of grazing rights. No less than 352 'old tenements' received small allotments on their various sides of the forest. Here again, though, the awards were made to the landowners, not the tenant farmers. The land was mostly made over in blocks, according to ownership, and remained thus—in any case the small parcels would hardly have been worth individual farming. Sir Charles Bampfylde received the largest slice of the cake, the sum total of ninety-eight distinct allotments appertaining to ninety-five tenants. One can certainly understand the feelings of the many small farmers.

The remainder of the Forest of Exmoor, some 10,262 acres in all, that central portion with Simonsbath House in its midst, and called now the King's Allotment, was offered in 1818 for sale by public tender. The highest bidder was Mr John Knight of Worcestershire. His offer of £50,000 made him owner of one of the last great stretches of open moorland in the south of England, and brought him the makings of a great estate. What he did with it belongs to another chapter.

THE ACLAND PONY HERD

Before finally leaving the subject of the old Royal Forest, one last word should be said about the ponies and their fate. Upon the disafforestation Sir Thomas Acland, the last warden of the forest, before relinquishing his wardenship, drove down from the forest the four hundred best ponies from the old herd and took them to Winsford Hill. Here they ran for many years, being managed from Old Ashway, and carrying the famous anchor brand. Of this Acland herd much has been said and written, and many of the best ponies of today derive from it.

As to the remainder of the forest ponies, they were sold off to various buyers and came down to mingle with others of their kind upon the commons of Exmoor. At least one well-known breeder of today traces the beginnings of his herd to ponies bought by his great-grandfather at the forest dispersal sale.

With regard to the number of ponies on the forest at the time of the disafforestation, there seems to exist no precise or definite statement. Billingsley is content to say 'upwards of four hundred', but since four hundred is the given number as driven off by Sir Thomas, the whole original herd must have been considerably 'upwards' of this, probably by several more hundreds.

5. THE KNIGHTS
AND SOME OTHERS

John Knight was a man of Worcestershire, descendant of a family of wealthy ironmasters, and a man of great vision, enterprise and energy. His worthy forbears had, by their qualities of intellect and vigour, accomplished many things in the spheres of industry, agriculture and art and had raised themselves to positions of honour and importance in their native Midlands. Though of a younger branch of the family, John Knight had behind him a heritage of enterprise and ambition, and many examples of the success that follows diligence.

PURCHASE OF EXMOOR FOREST

When the virgin untamed land of Exmoor Forest was offered for sale in 1818, some spark of vision, some spirit of the pioneer must have stirred within him, firing him with resolve to take and make what he could with this last wild wilderness of the Somerset moors. There was plenty to fire his dreams and ambitions, all around and beyond his own background, for it was an age of pioneers. Coke of Norfolk had made a great agricultural estate out of what had been but poor heathy waste. The dukes of Bedford had done great things in the Ouse valley; Bakewell of Dishley had in years past revolutionized the breeding of livestock; and, nearer at hand to Exmoor, the Quartlys of Molland had done great things with stock and performed wonders with their farmland. Among men a spirit of progress was kindling, and adventure too, for overseas the call of the bush, the veldt and the prairie was making itself heard in the hearts of the hardy settlers, moving dreamers with the whisper of the vast potentials.

John Knight thought, considered and acted. His bid of £50,000 for the so-called 'King's Allotment' proving the highest offer, he became in the August of 1818 the purchaser of the heart of Exmoor Forest.

His next act was to 'buy out' those neighbours who had acquired large slices of the old forest as awards in lieu of ancient rights. He purchased first Sir Charles Bampfylde's south-western allotment of 1,880 acres, and then Sir Thomas Acland's big north-eastern allotment of 3,200 acres, for which latter he paid 5,555 guineas. Both gentlemen already had large estates of settled lands, and no doubt were very willing to part with what was merely very rough moorland for what were then substantial prices. He bought also the manor of Brendon, which carried with it Sir Arthur Chichester's allotment, and several other smaller allotments as well. By 1820 he had acquired some 15,500 acres, in all nearly three-quarters of the whole area of the original forest.

Now the work of reclamation had to begin, and the long struggle of transforming the untamed wilderness into a worthy estate entered upon. It was a case of starting from scratch, for although the Crown Commissioners had marked out roads-to-be, and made provision for a future village at Simonsbath, there were in fact no roads at all over the forest, only very rough and scarcely discernible moorland tracks.

Owing to this lack of any proper highways, operations seem to have been started from Lynmouth. Here, where there was a small quay, supplies, equipment, stock, etc., could be brought in from the sea and unloaded ready for the assault on the moor.

BOUNDARY WALLS AND ROADS

John Knight's first work was the building of a strong stone boundary wall all round the perimeter of his land, completely encircling and enclosing it. In parts the wall followed the line of the original forest bounds, and some of the old markers were incorporated in it. Where the wall crossed the trackways gates were fixed, some of them ingenious double ones designed to clap against the wind in either direction. (The best known of these, Brendon Two Gates, is now replaced by a modern cattle-grid, while Honeymead and others have quite disappeared.) The wall was completed some time before 1824 and, needless to say, was not at first very popular with the hunting folk.

The next step was roads. As every true pioneer realizes, communications are the first essential of any campaign of conquest or construction. John Knight, as befits one of his character, was a great maker of roads. He first cut and metalled the old bridle tracks that radiated from Simonsbath to Lynmouth and Brendon, Exford, Sandyway and South Molton. Later on the road to Challacombe was made up. These good new roads must have been the wonder of the countryside. Up to this time there had been no road worthy of the name anywhere in the hill country of Exmoor, and not a wheeled vehicle to be seen north of Dulverton or west of Porlock. There seems to have been no obligation upon John Knight to make up the roads—he seems to have done this on his own initiative and from his own foresight.

LAND RECLAMATION

Access to the forest estate and its central house now being assured on three sides, the actual work of pioneer farming could begin. The natural sites for farmsteads were the south slopes of the hills that looked towards the sun, and the best land for cultivation the gradually levelling ground that ran back from them towards the wide tablelands of the hilltops. The long valley of the Barle, running mainly east-south-east, with wide gradual slopes in many of its parts, was the terrain selected by John Knight for his first experiments.

At Honeymead, east of Simonsbath, and at Cornham, westwards and upstream, the operations started. Here the land was of the 'dry' moorland sort, good brown loam over yellow sub-soil, with 'shillet'—loose slaty rock—beneath it. The natural herbage was mostly bent or 'forest grass', it being 'green' or grass-moor ground. The first task in this breaking of virgin soil was that of 'spading', whereby the top layer of turf was skimmed off with a broadshare. These turves were then gathered into heaps and burnt, and the ash spread upon the ground. Then the ground was limed and the ploughing began. Bullock teams of six oxen drew the ploughs. The method adopted was that of 'halving', whereby only alternate furrow widths were ploughed, each furrow slice turning up on to standing ground, so leaving the land in ridges. The earth was ploughed to the depth where it touched the subsoil, and where clay and 'iron-pan' appeared every second furrow was broken by subsoiling. The land was then left until the following spring, when it was 'worked' and sown. The success of this method, with its initial draining and weathering of the newly broken soil, can be gauged by the good heart of the fields today. At the same time that this work was under way, the Honeymead and Cornham farmsteads were being built, and must have been finished some time before 1828. Red Deer (later known as Gallon House) was also built and licensed as an inn.

One of the first things to be realized was the importance of lime in the acid moorland soil, and the provision of this was one of the major expenses of the undertaking. A thorough search was made upon Exmoor itself in the hope of finding limestone rocks, but with little success. Almost all the lime had to be hauled from Combe Martin, or from Newland near Exford, where there was an outcrop of lime-rock and a kiln.

FIRST CROPS AND STOCK

Having broken and prepared his first land, Knight proceeded to farm on the well-known four-course rotation, and here he made his first mistake. The climate of Exmoor, high, wild and wet, made virtually impossible what was essentially a low-country system. The dream of great fields of wheat and barley blowing golden on the high hills could be nothing but an illusion, yet John Knight with all his perspicacity seemed not to have realized this. He persisted in trying to grow corn crops (which, nine times out of ten, must have been wretched failures), until the day of his death.

For the time being the thousands of acres of untouched rough ground beyond the area of cultivation seem to have been used as in former times for the depasturing of agisted animals, but Knight was nevertheless very busy enclosing with walls large areas in preparation for his own future stock. He very well knew the value of good stock, and the importance of getting the best strains possible, and to this end made many journeys northwards—he was his own agent, and an indefatigable worker and traveller, and on one occasion (in 1826) made a record journey from Bristol to Carlisle in two nights and a day, leaving at evening and arriving on the morning of the second day. This was travelling indeed in those days of horses and coaches, and the expedition was but one of many.

About this time he bought West Highland bullocks (400) and Herefords (some 300), and brought his herds home to Exmoor. At first the Highlanders seemed to do well, and to acclimatize, but even they could not survive an Exmoor winter without some hand feeding (nothing can do that but the native ponies). Also they began to get a bad reputation for being wild and wicked—almost, it would seem, going wild like the feral cattle of the prairies. So in the end they had to go; but though one recognizes the necessity, one cannot but help wish that some had remained. What a sight they must have been, upon the tawny heights or in the swampy bogs, like buffalo come to life again! Eventually the Herefords went too, and the native Devon cattle took their place as of old.

With regard to sheep, Knight started off with Exmoors, but they did not satisfy him. He then brought in Cheviots from the north, but even they seem not to have pleased him. He next tried the experiment of a flock of a hundred merino ewes. What happened to them does not seem to be recorded; perhaps it is better so—one can hardly think of a more unsuitable breed for the country.

The sheep seem to have caused Knight a good deal of trouble at this stage. He had great difficulty in getting shepherds, which was understandable when one considers the immense solitude of the as yet unsettled moor, and as a result large numbers of the sheep died or were 'lifted' by unscrupulous folk. So bad did the poaching get that Knight formed a guard of immigrant Irishmen to patrol his boundaries and protect his property, but it would seem that these 'potato-eaters' had only one true interest in life, and that was fighting, either with others or amongst themselves. In the end they, like the wicked cattle, had to go.

An experiment in Westphalian pigs was tried. Knight's brother-in-law Lord Headley sent a number from Ireland. They came from Cork to Bristol, then by another ship to Ilfracombe, and from there were conveyed by cart to the wilds of Exmoor. The idea seems to have been that they should run wild in Brendon woods! Their ultimate fate history does not record.

HORSES

One of John Knight's chief livestock ventures was in the realm of horse-breeding. He had, upon the driving-down and dispersal of the old Exmoor Forest herd of ponies, bought from Sir Thomas Acland a considerable number of these native ponies. This part of the original herd came back to Simonsbath, and Knight set about 'improving' the breed according to his standards. Having heard good reports of the large size and impressive looks of the Dongola Arabs, he joined with several friends in the venture of importing some of these. Two stallions and three mares of this oriental breed duly arrived at Simonsbath. A portrait by James Ward of one of these Dongola stallions gives a fair idea of the general make and appearance of the animals—the painting shows a tall black horse, imposing and generally well made, but rather 'on the leg', with four white feet and a slightly Roman-nosed head. On the whole, such a cross seems quite unsuitable for local stock. Knight also brought in several thoroughbred sires and thoroughbred mares, and also thirty mares of Cleveland type.

From this mixture of equine stock he proceeded to breed horses and ponies of various sorts and sizes—hunters, hacks and harness horses—some of which were very good indeed, and some not so good. The hunters that he bred were reputedly the best in the neighbourhood. The Simonsbath stud was both pleasurable and profitable.

One thing, though, he learnt, as many others since have done, and this was that only uncrossed ponies of the old native stock could winter out untended and unfed on the desolate moor. No other breed could do this, and even with the native ponies themselves any sort of crossing, or any attempt to increase the size resulted in the loss of the amazing natural hardiness that had enabled them to survive from the prehistoric past. He found that first-cross mares could survive and rear foals only if they were overwintered in enclosed land on good grass.

THE CURSE OF HORSEMEN

As well as his agricultural experiments, Knight also did some less understandable things. The chief of these was the damming up of the headwaters of the Barle to form the now well-known Pinkery Pool. What his purpose could have been no one knows. Some sort of watercourse seems to have been planned to lead from it, heading towards Simonsbath, and it may be that he had in mind plans for irrigation, or some sort of water-power plant, but whatever it was it came to naught, for the work was never finished despite the employment of two hundred Irish labourers upon the job. He also cut drain ditches across some of the deep peat land in the hope (futile as it proved) of draining it, and these have been the curse of horsemen ever since.

In those first years of enthusiasm John Knight had resolved, or so it would seem, to devote the rest of his life and energy to the development of his Exmoor estate, and to reside at Simonsbath and manage the whole of the vast enterprise in demesne. To this end he began, at about the same time as he was breaking the first lands, to set the foundations of a fine mansion upon rising ground at Simonsbath, and to start dismantling his old midland home at Wolverly. Simonsbath Mansion, intended as the future family seat, was sited just behind and above Simonsbath House—probably it was intended to pull down the latter on completion of the former—and a considerable amount of building ensued, but the place was never finished, becoming, like many another of its sort, a large 'white elephant'; and ultimately the masonry shell was pulled down.

The road of reclamation was not smooth. The old forest was a harsh, resentful land, and John Knight made a number of mistakes in his dealings with it. His greatest error, the one which brought him constant failure, was his insistence on trying to force a midland pattern of farming on a hill country. He had been brought up to midland farming and could not, or would not, abandon its methods. He had financial failures too in other walks of life, and as he began to grow old he was no doubt wearied by his various troubles. In 1842, at the age of seventy-six, he resigned the management of the Exmoor estate to his eldest son, Frederick Winn Knight, and retired to Italy to spend the remainder of his days in Rome.

FREDERICK KNIGHT

Frederick Knight was a young man of great energy and capabilities. At the same time as he took over the Exmoor estate, he stood for Parliament and was elected Member for West Worcestershire. He remained an M.P. for forty-four years and in 1886 received the K.C.B. for public services, so becoming Sir Frederick Knight.

For a little while Frederick carried on along his father's lines, but it had already entered his mind that a better system of management would be to let the growing farms to tenants. Accordingly Honeymead and Simonsbath Barton were let off with 2,100 and 1,030 acres of land, on twelve-year leases at rents of £740 and £439 per annum respectively. The next lettings were Emmet's Grange, then in course of construction and, in 1844, Cornham. The tenants seems to have come from Wiltshire—men attracted by the low rents, and little knowing what was in store for them. The newcomer to Emmet's was a dairy-farmer, and after his first season he asked to be freed from his lease!

NEW FARMS

With four farms off his hands, young Knight continued with his task of enclosing large fields from the waste and establishing more farmsteads for prospective letting. By this time he had taken as his agent one Mogridge of Molland, a Devon man well versed in the farming of the region. Together they worked to bring more and more of the moor in hand. The general procedure seemed to be that of first enclosing suitable land, and then erecting the necessary buildings at a somewhat later date. The fields enclosed were large, some fifty acres or so (a very great contrast to the little five-acre fields of the old hill farms), but the walls about them were mostly high earthen banks of the traditional sort, faced with stone 'dyking' and topped with a spine of turf. An innovation was the cresting of these banks with young beech plants designed to grow into stock-proof wind-breaking hedges. (There were nurseries for the raising of the young beech plants from seed at Simonsbath.) What immense labour must have gone into the making of these miles of walls! What a slow and tedious job it must have been, clatting-up,[1]

[1] Making banks of sods of turf.

A TYPICAL 'KNIGHT' FARM WITH ITS WINDBREAK

setting the dyking, and finally planting and caring for the young
beech plants. Some of the walls, though, like the very first
encircling one and the one along Exe Cleeve, were of the
northern dry-stone sort, and suggest outside influence, probably
Irish.

The next farmsteads to be built and finished were Driver
(with 400 acres), Duredon (900 acres), Warren (700 acres),
Horsen (400 acres) and Wintershead (200 acres). Pinkery (400
acres) came later, and Larkbarrow, Tom's Hill, Winstitchen,
Cloven Rocks and Picketstones last of all. Titchcombe, though
designated, seems never to have materialized except as a
shepherd's cottage. All seem to have been completed by about
1852.

Knight and Mogridge seem to have been their own archi-
tects, using as much as possible local labour and materials.

Local stone was used for all the buildings, but Welsh slate was brought across (to Lynmouth harbour) for the roofing. The farmsteads followed for the most part the traditional hill-country layout, being grouped long and low about a central yard, the only concession to nineteenth-century enlightenment being that the houses were set facing outwards, not inwards to the yards. The buildings are all of extremely sound construction, almost fortress-like in their severity, and fit well into their environment, seeming by their very harshness to be in harmony with and to express the wild lonely spirit of the high moor. The houses themselves are of good proportions, and within have something of the dignity and spaciousness of that late Georgian age which first gave them being. About each group of buildings was planted a thick windbreak of beech or sycamore.

In 1848 a new figure appears on the scene, Robert Smith of Lincolnshire, who came to take over as agent. He was a man of wide agricultural experience and to him it was at once apparent that the midland corn-growing style of farming was quite unsuited to Exmoor. From his regime dates the gradual turn over to the now very successful roots-grass-and-stock policy of today. During his tenure, until 1866, he resided at Emmet's Grange.

With regard to the later-made farms, the fact had to be faced that the double expense of erecting buildings and enclosing land was putting a most severe strain on the economy of the estate. Therefore it was decided to let these last farms virtually unenclosed, finding tenants who, in return for certain concessions, would themselves make up the walls and banks, and break the virgin soil. This was done, and for a time all seemed well. The conditions of the leases, with stipulations for specific improvement on the one hand, and generous rebates for work done on the other, plus a rising scale of rent, seemed very fair to both landlord and tenant.

A notable tenant of round about this era was Gerard Spooner of Wintershead. He it was who first brought down Scottish

Blackface sheep to Exmoor, and Scottish shepherds and their collies to mind them. He also had Cheviots, which seem to have thrived very well in his hands.

About this time a visit was made to the Knight estate by Sir Thomas Acland. He seems to have been very impressed by all that he saw. He notes that the plantations were rising about the houses, that the roots and grass were doing well, also the stock, that the cattle were mostly Devons, and that some good cheese was being made in some of the farmhouses. The tenant of Cornham had a herd of Devon cross Hereford yearlings in fine condition. A sixty-acre field of purple-topped turnips at Horsen he thought the finest he had ever seen. Seven hundred Exmoor cross Southdown sheep were grazing on these turnips, and on the outer pastures a flock of Exmoor ewes were running with a Leicester ram.

SIMONSBATH AND MINING VENTURES

Meanwhile the little village of Simonsbath was struggling into existence. With its 'big house', Barton farm inn and various cottages it could now claim to be recognized as such and look forward to official status. Provision had been made at the disafforestation for the building of a church, and the creation of a parish of Exmoor when time and population should warrant this, and so in 1855 the foundations of Simonsbath church and parsonage were laid. The church was finished and consecrated the following year. The parsonage also was completed and furnished with ten acres of glebe, and the Rev. W. H. Thornton became the first incumbent. The church is a pleasant little place, plain and unassuming, and its yard is sunny and cheerful, quite unlike the majority of Victorian religious establishments. A village school was also built.

At the same time that he was busy with the agricultural development of Exmoor, Frederick Knight looked to the possibilities of mineral exploitation. The hills about Simonsbath were known to carry iron ore and possibly copper, and he embarked upon certain mining ventures. The first mine to come into being was the Wheal Eliza, near Flaxbarrow, operated under lease by a small company. It certainly contained some good iron ore, but eventually came to nothing. Further prospecting went on at Burcombe, Picketstones, Hangley Cleeve, Cornham and some other places, and, the indications seeming favourable, negotiations were entered into with the Dowlais mining company of Wales, and some others. There were even plans for a mineral railway to run from Simonsbath to Porlock. Eventually though, despite a good deal of capital having been sunk in the various undertakings, the whole business came to nothing and the shafts and workings were abandoned. Perhaps we should be glad that it was so, and that Exmoor was spared the scars of industrial development.

NEW METHODS OF FARMING

Old John Knight died in 1851, leaving Frederick in sole possession. At first things went on much as before, with little apparent change, but gradually the hard fact had to be faced that all was not well. Exmoor Forest is a harsh and intractable country, by no means easily tamed and, despite the splendid and (at first sight) profitable work that had been accomplished, more and more capital had to go into the business while less and less profit came out of it. One by one the tenants—none of them local men, they being 'up-country' folk who had been attracted by what had seemed in the beginning a profitable venture—got into difficulties and could not pay their rents, and eventually departed. Not one of the original tenants stayed more than a few years. The local hill farmers seem to have been highly amused at the plight of the strangers.

Robert Smith himself made a success of Emmet's Grange, having gone about things the right way. His method was to pare and burn the rough land, spread the ashes and add lime at about $2\frac{1}{2}$ tons to the acre, then plough—he preferred oxen to horses—and work and sow down to roots. The second year he sowed good grass, mixed with rape, which remained down for four or five years, when it was ploughed up for an oat crop. This gave a seven-year rotation, mostly grass, and proved to be one of the best for the land and climate. It is one still followed on many farms, except that oats have generally been given up. He claimed that his grass, if stocked in June, would fatten ten sheep to the acre.

Frederick Knight eventually gave up the hunter-breeding stud. Having found that none but the native ponies could winter naturally upon Exmoor, he no doubt found the expense of cosseting large numbers of half-breds through the long wet winters too much for his purse. He still kept a herd of some four hundred true Exmoors on the heights, though, and also maintained numerous hunters at Simonsbath for his own use. The Knight family were great lovers of hunting, and the Staghounds used to meet at Simonsbath on occasion. Frederick did what he could to preserve the wild red deer, though at this time their numbers had dropped very low. He also tried the experiment of introducing fallow deer. An enclosed deer park had been made, stretching up to Blue Gate—the area is still known as 'Deer Park'—and bucks and does installed. They did well enough, but would not be confined, and by continuously escaping did so much damage to crops that in the end they had to go.

For a while the affairs of the estate were not good. The tenant-farms were not paying, and the mining and other ventures had failed. The work of wholesale reclamation stopped and was never resumed. No more new farms were made, and the wild central heights, those desolate bog-crowned hills that are the heart of Exmoor, were left as they had always been, a summer pasturage for cattle and an empty loneliness in winter. With all one's admiration for the Knights and their work one must be glad that this was so, and that today we may walk over the roof of the moor and know it still in its primeval and unaltered state.

Then, gradually, farming affairs began to improve. Tenants were found for the farms—local men who understood the ways of the moor and its climate. They were bred to the hill country, and followed the traditional style of 'family farming', all members of the family from the small children upwards helping father with the various jobs. In their hands the forest farms began to improve and prosper at last, and have never gone back.

In 1866 Robert Smith retired and a new person came on the scene. He was Frederick L. Smyth, of Westlandpound Farm, to the west of the moor. Smyth had had a good deal of experience of moorland reclamation, having among other things successfully broken and cultivated a part of Challacombe Common that had fallen to him, and when he came to take up the position of agent upon the forest he brought with him the fruits of much acquired knowledge. His method of dealing with the difficult black peat-land was to pare, burn, lime and plough the ground, then sow at once to rape, and graze the rape off with sheep. This rape-and-sheep cropping was repeated for three or four consecutive years, then the ground was broken and subsoiled and sown down to permament pasture. The method answered well. The rape roots got deep down, the sheep fattened on the rape, and the growth and the sheep-treading decomposed the thick peat. The chief grasses used for sowing down were rye grass, timothy grass, cocksfoot and Yorkshire fog, together with perennial clovers. With regard to the latter it may be noted that wild white clover comes naturally on Exmoor pastures once a sward has been established.

SHEEP AND SCOTTISH SHEPHERDS

Frederick Knight resolved to experiment further with sheep. His main idea was to breed for mutton rather than wool, and to fatten his lambs on the new grass pastures. He tried first with a flock of five hundred Exmoor Horns on Winstitchen, but they did not winter well on the high ground, so, like his father, he turned to the north for some other more hardy breed.

From Scotland he brought down mountain Blackfaces and also another flock of Cheviots, and with them Scottish shepherds to be his flock-masters. The Blackfaces went first to Hoar Oak, then to Winstitchen, and then in drafts to each of the farms that fell vacant. Most of these sheep came by sea to the little port of Lynmouth, which was still the easiest approach to the heart of Exmoor, but the last flock, one of Cheviot ewes, was railed to Bristol and driven the eighty miles from there to Exmoor by a shepherd on foot. This was in 1871.

Both the sheep and their Scottish shepherds settled down well. The Cheviots especially throve, and were ultimately preferred to the Blackface. The practice was to keep the ewes until they were five years old, breeding to a ram of their own kind, then, in their last year, to cross them with a Leicester or Shropshire ram for a crop of large lambs. Both ewes and lambs fattened well on the rape and summer grass, and went off at the autumn sales in first-class condition. Some of the fat sheep were sold at Simonsbath direct to the butchers, and the rest were driven down to South Molton market. It was the policy to be rid of all such stock before November if possible, because of the difficulty of providing winter keep. About this time Knight experimented with kale, then a new crop in England, hoping that it might be a good frost-resistant stand-by.

As for the Scottish shepherds, they became part of the Exmoor scene and traditions. They stayed, and their children and grandchildren became men of the moor. Today the third generation of one family, the Littles, farm several of the farms in Exford parish, and are settled down as West Countrymen. The northern sheepdogs stayed too, and the lean working collies of today, black and white, black and tan, and occasionally red, are probably descendants of this worthy stock.

By the 1870's machinery had started to make its appearance

upon the land. Frederick Knight made use of mowing machines and other horse-drawn implements for his hay crops, and then in 1876 resolved to give steam-power a trial for heavy reclamation work. The tackle selected was Messrs Fowler's Sutherland steam plough. This consisted of an engine that worked on a comparatively small amount of coal and a great deal of water, with a heavy double-ended plough mounted on rollers and having furrow shares underneath, and subsoiling shares or hooks at either end. The massive plough was pulled to and fro on anchored cables. The furrows it made were huge, a foot deep and two feet wide, and the subsoilers when let down could break the ground to a depth of three feet. How such tackle could ever have reached the Exmoor wilds, and what its travels and adventures through the narrow lanes and up and down the steep hills and around the narrow bends must have been, is something one's mind boggles over even now. Arrive it did, though, and seems to have justified its existence by doing some good work. At Titchcombe some four hundred acres of deep wet peat land were successfully broken and drained by the monster, and later more ground at Duredon and Prayway was tackled.

By this era too the railway had reached out westwards from Bristol to Taunton, and then to Barnstaple via Dulverton and South Molton. This made transport and marketing of commodities an easier matter and reduced the former importance of Lynmouth as a port.

The year 1880 or thereabouts marks the high tide of the Exmoor Forest farming. As much land as seemed profitable had been developed, and a balance arrived at between cultivated land and rough grazing. Some of the unimproved ground on the outlying parts of the estate, such as Long Hoccombe, was let off to outside farmers for summer bullock pasture. For the rest, Frederick Knight went over more and more to sheep-farming. Some cattle were maintained, but the ponies were reduced to a mere forty head, and as certain farms came in hand he kept and maintained these as sheep-herdings. Eventually these numbered eight, namely Larkbarrow, Tom's Hill, Hoar Oak, Pinkery, Duredon, Cornham, Winstitchen and Wintershead.

Cropping only for sheep-keep, his rotation tended to be rape and turnips, then rape and seeds, the resultant grass ley staying down for as long as it remained good. When this was broken again a crop of oats for horse-feed might be taken, but gradually the growing of oats was discontinued because of the persistently bad wet harvests. Likewise turnips began to give way to the rape, which throve wonderfully. He made both hay and silage for winter keep, and wintered his ewes in the enclosures, but the best of the lambs were sent down off the moor to the neighbourhood of Dunster for the winter months.

A number of Shorthorn heifers were brought in to keep company with the Devons, and seem to have done well enough. Several teams of heavy horses were maintained for working and hauling, principally Suffolk Punches, though he also had Percherons. Some of the Suffolks were actually bred on the place, for he kept a stallion for this purpose.

Despite all his ups and downs and setbacks, Frederick Knight had done well, and he might have done even greater things had not his only son died suddenly, in 1879, at the age of twenty-seven. The blow was a mortal one from which he never really recovered, though with fortitude and courage he tried to carry on for a while. At last, in 1897, he too departed this life, and the saga of the Knights was at an end.

When John Knight bought the major part of the old forest in 1818 it had been an empty wilderness with but one house and a small farm, and five people dwelling therein. The income of the whole was reckoned at about £350. As Frederick Winn Knight left it, some sixty years later, it was an estate carrying fifteen good moorland farms, and a village supporting a population of nearly three hundred persons and returning a gross rental of about £4,500. At the time of his death Knight had in hand some 9,000 acres, and some 9,000 head of sheep, plus a number of cattle and some horses.

THE FORTESCUES

Following the death of his son and heir, and having no other child, Frederick Knight had sold the reversion of his estate to Earl Fortescue of Castle Hill. These rights the earl transferred to his son, Lord Ebrington, and the latter entered into possession of the Exmoor Forest estate about two months after Sir Frederick Knight's death. Now the forest entered into yet another phase of its history, for with the vast extent of the Castle Hill lands all lying on good north Devon ground below the line of the moors, joined to it and available for the seasonal transfer of stock, the old Knight pattern of things became outmoded. The new policy was mainly to let off to tenants as much of the forest land as possible, and to use the remainder for summering stock from lower ground. Six of the sheep-ranching herdings were retained in hand, however, and the forest Cheviots remained as a continuing enterprise. These sheep were the direct descendants of those Cheviots brought from Scotland by Frederick Knight, having been taken over at valuation. Some 5,000 ewes and a hundred rams were retained, and later it became the custom to take them down to the 'better ground' at Castle Hill for the winter months. Under the Fortescue regime all tenants were men born and bred on Exmoor, men who knew well how to make the best use of the high forest ground. Their cattle were Red Devons, and the sheep they kept mostly Exmoors.

In 1933 the Fortescue Estate tried a new experiment—the introduction of black Galloway cattle to the forest. Ten cows and a bull were the first comers. They did well on the high rough ground, being extremely hardy, and the numbers were increased. Bulls of various kinds were tried for a first cross, including a white Shorthorn for the well-known 'blue-grey' cross, but in the end a Hereford was considered to give the best results (How startled I was on one occasion when coming up through the deep cotton-grass to the Chains and, seeing black cattle grazing before me, I was suddenly confronted with a rank of staring skull-white faces!) The pure Galloway can winter out, growing a coat like a shaggy bear, and needs only to have food thrown to it in very hard weather. There are, I believe, some hundred-odd Galloway cows now kept on the forest, some for breeding pure and some for crossing.

Up till 1927 the Knight-Fortescue Exmoor Forest Estate had remained intact, but in that year four farms—Honeymead, Winstitchen, Picketstones and Red Deer—were sold away to Sir Robert Waley-Cohen. For good or ill the days of great estates were passing.

A few years ago, as a result of the death of the late Earl Fortescue in 1958, the Fortescue Estate was parted up. Portions of the estate were sold off, including Emmet's Grange, Winters-head and Pinkery, but a good deal still remains in Fortescue hands.

The work of John Knight and his son Frederick had far-reaching effects on Exmoor as a whole, beyond the bounds of their own estate, for it stimulated interest in land improvement and reclamation over a wide area.

ENCLOSURE OF THE COMMONS

In the south-west portion of the forest, on those allotted lands which had not fallen into the possession of John Knight, another group of new farms came into being. These and their enclosures were carved out by certain other landlords who seem to have been no less busy on their smaller lands than John Knight was on his greater estate. These new farms were: Kinsford, Higher Sheardon, Lower Sheardon, Ferny Ball, Woolcombe, Sandyway, Barkham, Lytton, Willingford and Green Barrow. (The last named, a small place on the Withy-pool–Sandyway road, has now quite gone down, and its traces can be discerned only by someone who knows where to look.)

An inn, now called The Sportsman's Arms, was also built. It stands by the crossroads at the county boundary, and has become well known as a meeting place of both the staghounds and the foxhounds.

A less happy result of the urge for land reclamation was the ultimate enclosure of many of the commons. The high enterprise of the Knights no doubt fired the ambitions of various lesser local men, who then cast covetous eyes on the wide expanses of moorland still within their own parishes. Under the pressure and influence of these would-be magnates, various Acts were passed, between 1841 and 1872, for the enclosure of no less than thirty-one open commons (*see* Appendix E).

These enclosures of common land, advantageous though they might be to the larger farmers and landowners, struck heavily at the 'little men', with little farms or holdings, or folk with just 'cottage right'. The larger man received a substantial allotment which, when enclosed, could be turned to good use, but the little man received at best a few acres which were in themselves no recompense for the loss of extensive grazing rights and often, having neither the time nor money for actual fencing, he lost even that little which was given him. By the 1860's a rising tide of public opinion called a halt to the wholesale and indiscriminate enclosure of moorland, and after the end of that decade no more enclosure Acts were passed, the Wootton Courtenay Awards being the last to be made.

THE FIRST CARTS

Apart from the work of enclosure and reclamation, the most noteworthy happening of the time was the introduction of carts into the hill country. The first carts began to appear on the hill farms in the 1830's, and were as great an innovation then as the motor-car was in more recent times. As before this the country had known only sledges and pack-horses, the coming of wheeled vehicles must have been quite revolutionary and something to be marvelled at in the high hills. From places as far apart as Martinhoe, Withiel Flory, Withypool and Exford, the time is not long gone when the oldest inhabitants could remember the coming of the first carts. The first cart ever to come into Withypool is said to have arrived on a Sunday morning, whereupon all the good folk came out of church to see this remarkable thing. It would seem that the cart had been ordered by a very progressive farmer, a certain Mr Quartly (probably a relative of the Quartlys of Molland) who then resided at Weatherslade farm, and that it had come with much difficulty all the way from a township beyond the Brendons— Carhampton, I believe.

Tradition does not say what kind of carts these first vehicles were, but most probably they were of the small two-wheeled sort that were, until recently, in general use on all Exmoor farms. These little hill-country harvest carts, known in west Somerset as 'rail carts', and in north Devon as 'long-tail carts', consisted of a long wagon-like bed, with neatly railed sides, mounted on two wheels, and having the shafts going right through so as to form part of the structure. Lades were fixed fore and aft when hay and corn were carried. They were pleasing and graceful to look at, and manœuvred easily in the narrow ways and about the sharp turns of the hill country.

As roads improved, bigger four-wheeled wagons, drawn by teams of horses, came into general use for heavy transport, and gigs and carriages also appeared. In the course of time, following upon the example of the Knights, some fine new roads were made, wide and level, and in great contrast to the old narrow scored-out lanes. One interesting example is the highway from Chibbet Post to Exford, where the old and new roads run parallel, the former appearing like a deep ditch beside the latter, for a considerable distance.

TOURISTS AND HOLIDAY FOLK

Meanwhile, another sort of enterprise, and a pioneering very different from agriculture, was taking place along the northern sea coast of the moor—the first beginnings of the holiday business.

Exmoor in general, and the little coastal villages of Lynton, Lymouth and Porlock in particular, were first 'discovered' by tourists about the end of the eighteenth and beginning of the nineteenth centuries, during the period of the Napoleonic Wars. It was these last that were the chief cause of travellers from other parts of England finding their way to such hitherto remote and unknown spots, for Napoleon's campaigns closed most of Europe to English travellers for many years, with the result that those folk with the money and taste for touring had to find romantic scenery and congenial resorts nearer home.

Lynton and Lynmouth, small and remote under the towering hills, certainly suited the romantic taste of the period and delighted those who ventured so far westwards over the pack-horse tracks. Contemporary illustrations show Lynmouth as a tiny unsophisticated fishing village with its few cottages grouped between the foot of the wooded hill and the pebbly beach, whilst a fine two-arched bridge spans the hurrying waters of the Lyn and makes a pleasing focal point. Lynmouth at the time existed on herring fishing and small imports of lime and culm.

Shelley came to Lynmouth in 1812, and lived for a while in the cottage which now bears his name. Gainsborough also visited the village, and thought it a most delightful place, especially for a landscape painter. The poet Southey declared Lynmouth one of the finest places he had ever seen, and was loud in praise for its romantic beauty of rocky hills, deep woods and rushing rivers. Farther along the coast Porlock also was having its share of attention. Coleridge stayed at the Ship Inn, and local tradition credits his writing part of his *Kubla Khan* while there. Wordsworth too stayed at Porlock.

Steadily the numbers of tourists increased as the beautiful coast became better known and its fame noised abroad. Soon it became necessary to make special provision for the visitors.

Hotels came into being—Lynmouth's first hotel was built in 1807—and cottages were fitted up for letting. The Exmoor coast had become a holiday area!

The need for improved roads and transport soon became apparent. The only highway to and from the east was the old riding track over Countisbury Hill to Porlock, very bad in the winter, while those going on to Barnstaple were such as have already been described. Most connections were by sea, small coastal vessels unloading cargoes of lime, culm and passengers wherever there was sufficient beach for boats to come in, and a cliff path leading to the land above.

COACHES

At last, towards the middle of the century, the coast road from Porlock was made up for wheeled vehicles and visitors were able to arrive in proper style. Great was the rivalry of the hotels at Lynton (they numbered three in 1856), when the carriages of the wealthy were espied descending Countisbury Hill into Lynmouth! Preliminary observation having been made by telescope, post-boys were dispatched forthwith to meet the well-to-do tourists at the foot of Lynton Hill with extra horses for the final ascent, and to make quite sure the newcomers came to the correct hotel!

In or about 1850 the first coach service began, operating from Williton and reaching Lynmouth via Minehead and Porlock. At first the service was for the summer months only, but when the route became thoroughly established the coaches ran all the year, daily in the summer and once a week during the winter. So began the famous Porlock–Lynmouth coach run, so beloved by a former generation and still remembered by very many today. Three coaches were maintained, the Lorna Doone, the Red Deer and Katerfelto, each of which was drawn by a team of four strapping horses. For the long hard pull up Porlock Hill in the one direction, and up Countisbury on the return journey, a pair of cock-horses with postilion were attached, making six in all. Even so it was a struggle to surmount these two tremendous hills, and at the beginning of each hill, in order to lighten the coach, all male passengers were requested to get out and walk. A little farther on (and this story has been told before, I know, but it is here given as related to me first hand by a friend who remembers the occurrence), another request was made that 'all ladies under forty would get out and walk'. This usually had the effect of emptying the coach of *all* female passengers!

The journey from Lynmouth to Minehead (this being the point from which the service operated after 1874) took three hours, and the horses were changed at Culbone Stables some three miles from the top of Porlock Hill. On a fine summer's day the drive must have been a delight and a joy, but in winter it could be very grim without a doubt. At all times, though, the coach must have presented a splendid sight, gaily painted and loaded with passengers and luggage, and drawn by its four or six fine horses. The countryside through which it passed was then unspoiled, high open heather moor with here and there small farms and green high-banked fields, and all the way the blue of the sea on one hand and the depth of wooded valleys on the other. This was probably the finest coach route in southern England, and a noble approach to a delightful resort. (Alas, the old coaching road is now but a portion of the wired-in tarmac A.39 highway, along which the motor traffic of today tears at appalling speed.) The Lynmouth coach service was maintained until 1922, when it was superseded at last by motor-bus service.

During the latter part of the nineteenth century other coach services had come into being, linking Lynton and Lynmouth with Barnstaple and Ilfracombe. By 1880 the Lynton–Barnstaple service was running three return journeys a day during the summer. Its big four-horse coaches, the Royal Mail and the Glen Lyn, carried twenty passengers apiece, and the time for the route was just under three hours. The Lynton–Ilfracombe service was operated by the three coaches, the Tally-Ho!,

The Foresters and Benita, the last of which was noted for its fine team of grey horses. The first of these services was ended by the coming of the railway and the second by the advent of the buses.

LYNTON RAILWAY

It was the coming of the railways that opened up the country generally to the holiday maker. The first stretch of the Devon and Somerset Railway, from Taunton to Wiveliscombe, was opened in 1871, and two years later, in 1873, was continued thence to Barnstaple. In 1874 the Taunton–Minehead line was opened, and in the same year the Barnstaple railway was extended to Ilfracombe. This gave direct access to the Exmoor country from the south, east and west. On the Taunton–Barnstaple line Dulverton, East Anstey, Molland and South Molton now had their own stations and enjoyed a contact with the outside world such as they had not had before.

Lynton and Lynmouth, meanwhile, were not content with the proximity of the railways east and west of them, and desired a more direct link. It came in 1898 with the completion of Exmoor's very own line: the Lynton and Barnstaple Railway.

This delightful little railway, so completely in accord in all its ways and character with the nature of the hill country, was begun in 1895. It was designed as a single line narrow-gauge railway—the actual gauge was two feet—the better to negotiate the bends, curves and gradients imposed by the difficult terrain of western Exmoor. The route was from Barnstaple town station, by way of Chelfham, Bratton Fleming, Blackmoor Gate, Parracombe, Martinhoe Cross and so to Lynton. The laying of the line was itself a considerable engineering feat, for not only did the track have to thread its way snake-wise amongst the hills but it had to be carried across valleys in several places by viaducts. The biggest and finest of these was at Chelfham, where the line was carried high over a tributary of the Yeo upon a viaduct of eight graceful arches. (This still stands, and is a beautiful piece of architecture in its own right.) Everything to do with the little line was excellently constructed, bridges and station buildings alike being built of local stone expertly handled.

After three years the work was finished and all was ready for the opening. Commemorative medals had been struck ready for distribution to school children. At last the great day came. On the morning of 11th May 1898 the first train set forth for Lynton, having aboard the Mayor and Corporation of Barnstaple and other dignitaries. At Bratton Fleming a triumphal arch had been erected over the line, and the train was met with an address of welcome delivered on behalf of the parish. On arrival at Lynton the train was greeted with great enthusiasm, and after more speeches the Corporation of Barnstaple and the Lynton Urban Council proceeded to the Valley of Rocks Hotel for a grand luncheon. The railway was to run for thirty-seven years and to become part of the Exmoor story.

The service was maintained by five miniature engines: Yeo, Exe, Taw, Lew and Lyn. Each of these was fitted with a 'cow-catcher' for dealing with possible livestock obstruction on the line, and all presented a proper and general 'Wild West' appearance. A complete set of miniature rolling-stock was maintained: carriages (with first- and third-class compartments, guard and luggage compartments, and a dog-box!), goods vans, trucks, flats and a brake van. There were also inspection trolleys operated by hand.

As for the line itself, nature in its fecundity soon healed the scars made by the cuttings and embankments, sowing them with vegetation of all sorts. A journey on the little railway, especially in early summer, became a joy and a delight. How childhood memories reach back to such a day! I remember the swaying of the little carriages as the train jogged out of Barnstaple—owing to the very narrow gauge the coaches had a pleasant, slightly rolling motion not unlike that of a boat—and the excitement as it mounted to the hills. One leaned out of the window in delight as it rounded the big curves, and held one's hands out to the foliage (enthusiasts claimed they could pick flowers on the Lynton line!) and sniffed the clear sea air. The approach to the big viaduct was a period of anticipation, and the moments upon it a blissful thrill, for the train seemed to soar like a bird over the valley, and one looked down upon the ribbon of stream and the roofs and chimney-pots of the cottages below. The little stations came and went, and banks grew luxuriant with flowers of many kinds, the streams rushed alongside. One's view was untrammelled by hedges and un-spoilt by buildings. As the journey progressed the countryside grew wilder, and there was heather on the banks and thickets of gorse and fern everywhere. At the halts passengers gossiped, chickens patrolled the platforms and the guard walked out on to the road to see if any latecomers were hurrying for the train. If the train slowed up during the run (which it frequently did), one guessed there were stock on the line. By the time Parra-combe was reached one was up to Exmoor proper and could see the high moor. Then, oh joy! the blue of the sea, and at last one was in the small Lynton station high up on the hill, and here was journey's end. The journey itself, I think, took about an hour and a half.

Many are the tales told of the Lynton line: of the frequent encounters with cattle and sheep on the line, and sometimes with deer; of the time when a pig got on the track and refused to move; of the train stopping and the driver pointing out to the passengers a herd of deer that had just crossed the line. Once the train itself got mislaid (this was told to me by the same friend who remembered the coaching incident). At certain stations the engine had to uncouple for shunting, and on this particular occasion—it was at Bratton Fleming, I think—the driver forgot to hitch up again, with the result that on arrival at Barnstaple he found that he had left the train somewhere back up the line! My own favourite memory, though, is of the chickens that were kept by the stationmaster at one of the little stations (I am not quite sure which one). By day these chickens ranged far and wide, but when the approach of the train was heard, they with one accord made a concerted rush on to the platform, and as the train pulled in they hopped on to the running-board and into the opening doorways of the carriages. Experience had taught them that passengers left crumbs!

BUSES

Alas, like so many things that are pleasing and useful, the Lynton line did not pay. The running and maintenance costs were high, and by the 1920's the newly organized bus services—which could pick up folk almost off their own doorsteps—were drawing passengers away from it. Every year the railway continued to lose money. So at last in 1935 the Southern Railway company decided to close the line. It was a sad day when the little train ran for the last time, and sad when the small stations were dismantled and the rails pulled up and the track left to lapse into a memory. But the little Lynton line will never be forgotten, for it was and is a part of Exmoor.

Bus services began to operate over various parts of Exmoor during the 1920's. They too fitted into the life and pattern of the countryside and became part of it. Life was less hectic, time mattered not so much as it does today, and it was usual to wait about a bit for local passengers who might not have quite finished their breakfasts. Great care was always taken to see that return passengers were all aboard by the last bus home, and that they were each put out as near as possible to their own doorsteps. Sometimes there were other diversions. I remember one route where, upon summer evenings, a lookout was kept by the conductor for rabbits. If they were sighted, the bus stopped, and the conductor and driver, armed with sticks and stones and accompanied by as many of the passengers as cared to join in, attempted to gang up on the rabbits. I cannot remember many rabbits being bagged, but it was good fun! Mushrooms were another thing for which a watch was kept, and here the travellers were often more lucky! Happy days! Life is not what it was.

THE LIFE OF THE VILLAGE

Exmoor village life during the nineteenth and early twentieth centuries progressed much as in any other part of the country. Each small community was largely self-supporting, with blacksmith, wheelwright, carpenter, cobbler, baker and storekeeper, etc., serving the needs of the outlying hill farms and their folk. It was not until the coming of the motor-car, which gave direct access to the larger townships, that this local self-sufficiency declined. As to education, this came slowly to the hill country, firstly with small private and church schools, and then with the council schools: as, for instance, at Withypool, where the council school was built in 1877 and opened the following year with a first attendance of eighty pupils. (The schoolmaster's salary was fixed at the princely sum of £1 per week!) Prior to this there was a tiny private school in the village, held in one room of the local storekeeper's house, and for the privilege of attending this children paid twopence a week.

DEVON AND SOMERSET STAGHOUNDS

The Devon and Somerset Staghounds were established in 1855 to take the place of the old north Devon pack which had come to an end in 1825. During the interim period the country had been hunted intermittently by visiting staghound packs, but this arrangement had not been very satisfactory and, by the middle of the century, certain local gentlemen were desirous of establishing a resident pack once more. Chief amongst these was Dr Collyns of Dulverton, who had known and hunted with the old hounds in his youth, and it was largely owing to his efforts and enthusiasm that the new pack was got together and put on a proper footing.

The new pack was made up of drafts of large foxhounds, and was put into the field under the mastership of Mr Fenwick

Bissit, with Jack Babbage appointed as huntsman. The first two years were difficult, as hounds were new to their work and the deer had suffered much from the depredations of the poacher. (With regard to the latter it is possible that the organizing of this new resident pack came just in time to save the wild red deer of Exmoor from extinction, for their numbers had sunk to a very low level.) Gradually, though, everything settled down and the new hunt began to move forward to what was to be another brilliant period of staghunting. Mr Bissit remained master for twenty-five years, but in his time had many setbacks such as would have daunted any lesser man. At first the deer were few and the poachers many, and he had to carry on a ceaseless war against the latter. Financial worries were ever present as in previous times. Then in 1878 an outbreak of rabies occurred at the kennels, so that despite every effort to stamp this out the whole pack had to be destroyed. This was a heartbreaking occurrence, but fresh drafts of hounds were at once got together and hunting continued as usual the next season. The deer, however, began gradually to increase in numbers, and indeed before the end of his term of mastership had become so numerous, particularly in the Horner coverts, that it was necessary to hunt most persistently in order to keep them down.

Hounds were at first kennelled at Jury, then later, in 1861, moved to Rhyll, which at that time belonged to Mr Bissit. Both these places were inconvenient in that they were situated on the lower edge of the country, necessitating hounds having to 'lie out' at such places as Larkbarrow or Holnicote when their sport took them to the more northerly parts. So eventually it was decided to build new kennels at a more central point, namely Exford. The work on the new Exford kennels was started in 1875, and the buildings were finished and occupied the following year.

It was about this time that the fame of staghunting upon Exmoor began to spread beyond the bounds of the immediate country and to attract sporting visitors from more distant parts. Hitherto the hunting of the deer had been largely the sport and interest of local landowners, but now outsiders began to come in ever-increasing numbers to enjoy the thrill of the chase of the wild stag over the high open moor and to delight in the vigorous life of the hills.

Many small places shared in the prosperity brought by the hunting. Exford, with its kennels on the hill, became a small metropolis of the hunting world. Dulverton and Porlock were soon full of stables and the like. The inns and hotels everywhere were busy, and local properties were bought as hunting boxes. Every village street rang with hooves, and there was plenty of work for the saddlers and shoeing-smiths. About this time too Cloutsham became fixed as the place of the annual opening meet, it being the most convenient point for the now well-populated Horner coverts.

A ROYAL VISIT

The greatest day in the annals of the Devon and Somerset was that of the August morning in 1879 when Edward, Prince of Wales—later Edward VII—came up to Exmoor to hunt with the staghounds. The meet for that memorable morning was fixed at Hawkcombe Head, and thither forgathered the greatest assembly of foot and horsemen ever seen upon the moor. From every direction they came, from miles around, members of every hunt and every notable family in the West Country. The great concourse of people was estimated at something between 10,000 and 15,000, and the horsemen between 1,200 and 1,500. The day did not disgrace itself, for the sun shone, brilliant after a preceding night of rain, and the heather blazed purple in the morning light. It must have been a magnificent scene, with all the splendour of fine horses and handsome carriages and red coats in the sun, and the big hounds—fifteen couple of great dog-hounds—grouped in the midst of them all. The prince arrived in an open carriage, drawn by four horses with postilions in scarlet jackets. He was accompanied by Parson Jack Russell, Mr Luttrell, Prince Louis of Battenberg and Lord Charles Beresford. After the royal party had mounted their horses, hounds moved off. They kennelled at Culbone Stables, and the tufters were taken to the plantations. The stag that had been harboured there, however, refused to break covert—which was hardly to be wondered at in the circumstances—and so a move was made to the Deer Park above Badgeworthy. The pack was taken on to Larkbarrow.

In Deer Park the tufters soon roused a fine stag and the pack was laid on in Badgeworthy. With a great cry they raced away over the hill to Brendon Two Gates, on over the forest wall and across the heavy ground of Exe Plain. Here the stag turned northwards down the Hoaroak Water, continued below the shepherd's cottage, then went up over the Cheriton Ridge, down into Farley Water and out across the Brendon road. Now hounds were pressing him hard and he dropped to Badgeworthy again and turned up the little water—the so-called Doone Valley—and there stood at bay. The prince, piloted by Jack Russell and Mr Snow of Oare, had ridden well up with the hounds all the way and now was invited to give the *coup de grâce* with the huntsman's knife. This he did with a skill and resolution that drew admiration from the onlookers. It was reckoned that about five hundred horsemen in all came in to the finish, many of them galloping, scrambling and tumbling down the precipitous hillsides into the deep valley in their eagerness to be there at the end. Afterwards the prince and his party rode down to Badgeworthy with Nicholas Snow to take tea at Oare Manor before returning to Dunster. So ended a memorable Exmoor day.

When Lord Ebrington took over the mastership from Mr Bissit in 1881 the Devon and Somerset Staghounds were thoroughly established, the deer plentiful, the sport widely popular and the future of staghunting well assured. Under a succession of masters, such as Mr Basset, Mr Hornby, Colonel

Wiggan, etc., and huntsmen such as **Arthur Heal**, **Anthony Huxtable**, **Ernest Bawden** and **Sidney Tucker**, this ancient sport continued to flourish and prosper and to continue into our own time. Except for the interruption of the two world wars, whose years dislocated the lives and ways of all during those bitter times, there has been no break in the continuity of the Devon and Somerset Staghounds and their hunting of the wild deer of Exmoor between then and now.

Despite all the troubles and difficulties of a changing world, and thanks to the efforts of a number of devoted and determined men, we have our sport still, and the cry of the hounds to hearten us in the mornings, and the sight of the deer to gladden our eyes at sundown.

FOXHOUNDS AND HARRIERS

Before leaving the subject of hunting it is only fair to mention the several packs of foxhounds that have hunted over the moor. Foxes have always been abundant in the hill country, and it had been the practice in the eighteenth and earlier part of the nineteenth century for gentlemen having their own private packs of foxhounds to bring them up to Exmoor periodically to enjoy a chase over the high moor.

This was the age of the sporting parsons, and a number of West Country churchmen, as well as the local gentry, kept hounds of some sort, particularly in north Devon. Two names at once spring to mind, both closely associated with Exmoor: Parson Jack Russell of Swimbridge and Parson Froude of Knowstone. Of them many tales are told, good and bad, enough to fill a book on their own. Both hunted much on Exmoor with foxhounds and with harriers, and the cry of their hounds must often have echoed along the steep cleeves and in the goyals, and roused the farm folk from their work.

In the later part of the nineteenth century Nicholas Snow, the Squire of Oare, kept a fine pack of foxhounds kennelled at Oare Manor. These, the famous 'Stars of the West', hunted the heart of the moor, and were (I believe) the first truly resident pack of Exmoor foxhounds.

EXMOOR PONIES

In 1922 the Exmoor Pony Society was founded for the preservation and maintenance of this most ancient equine breed in its accepted original form. The standards fixed by the society were that ponies should not exceed 12·2 hands, should be bay, brown or dun (the Exmoor dun is a dark smoky brown having no resemblance at all to the light buckskin dun of other breeds), with no white markings whatsoever, and should always show the mealy muzzle and 'toad eye' so characteristic of the race.

Gradually, through the good work of the society and the efforts of numerous devoted breeders, the remarkable qualities of the true Exmoor pony—great strength, incredible hardiness, soundness and surefootedness—have become known far beyond the limits of its native home, and in recent years many of these 'little horses' have been exported to such far distant countries as Holland, Denmark, Norway, Sweden and Canada.

TAILPIECE:

EXMOOR TODAY

So now we reach the present day. Looking round, we see a country balanced between agriculture and the needs of tourists, sportsmen, naturalists and divers others.

Farming today is prosperous. The various grants and subsidies of recent years have helped to put hill farming on a firm footing, and almost all farms are now fully mechanized, with good access roads and modern conveniences of all sorts. The Land Rover goes everywhere, the tractor drones, and in the evening the hum of the generator tells of the lights and the 'telly' turned on. It is a far cry from the packhorse days.

Many new breeds have come to the moor to rival the native stock—the Devon Closewool (evolved from a cross between the Exmoor Horn and the Devon Longwool), the Scottish Blackface, the Cheviot, the Clun, the Dorset Down, the Welsh Mountain and some others, also Galloway cattle and some Herefords, plus miscellaneous beasts. Yet the native horn sheep and the Red Devon cattle still hold their own.

The trend of modern farming is towards enlarged holdings and the amalgamation of farms. Economic pressures make this necessary, but it is unfortunate, for by it many of the smaller farms are swallowed up and cease to exist. One of the sad things of the past half-century or so is the 'going down' of so many of the small, ancient farmsteads. Everywhere you may find their remains, sometimes no more than a few broken walls or a knot of trees to mark their past being.

Of wild life we still have an abundance. The lordly wild red deer seem to be on the increase rather than otherwise, and if we have lost the wild cat and the marten, at least we still have the fox, the badger, the otter and the hare. Exmoor is rich in bird life, and one may still see the raven, also the buzzard, the kestrel, the merlin and even rarer hawks in the sky, and hear the call of the curlew and the voice of the blackcock. The rivers too still hold their salmon and their trout.

Today, in addition to the Devon and Somerset Staghounds, the Exmoor country is hunted by four packs of foxhounds—the Exmoor Foxhounds (successors to the 'Stars of the West'), the Dulverton West, the Dulverton East and the West Somerset— and by the Minehead Harriers who, despite their name and green coats, hunt fox. Of recent years there had been a revival of the old practice of welcoming an outside pack to the moor, inasmuch as the Heythrop hounds have each season been invited to come and hunt on the moor for a few weeks in April.

Hares are fairly numerous on certain parts of the moor, and until recently there were two resident harrier packs: The Quarme Harriers and the Minehead Harriers. The former (who were kennelled at Exford) ceased to hunt during the last war, whilst the latter turned to fox round about the same time. The only hare-hunting to be had on Exmoor today is when the Crowcombe Basset hounds or some visiting pack of beagles come up for an occasional day on the moor.

Of late years the tourist trade has become what is possibly Exmoor's largest industry, rivalling perhaps even farming itself. With the improvement of roads and the general use of the motor-car, more and more people find their way into the hill country, some for short transitory stays, and some for more lengthy holidays. It is curious how Blackmore's romance *Lorna Doone*, based on the old legends of the moor (*see* page 88), has captured public imagination. Many people coming from far and wide tend to think of Exmoor as 'Lorna Doone' country, and those places specifically associated with the tale, such as Oare and Badgeworthy Water, undoubtedly draw more visitors than any other parts.

As to the railways, with the rise of road traffic and the greater convenience thereof, their importance has waned and they have declined. The year 1966 saw the closing of the Taunton–Barnstaple line, which from its stations of Dulverton, Anstey and Molland so long served the southern part of the moor. Today Exmoor's only railway link is Minehead, and even that remaining branch line is constantly threatened with closure.

In 1954 Exmoor was under Act of Parliament declared a National Park. This was the final step in the realization that here was a country whose wide stretches of open moorland, abundant wild life and great natural beauty, were such as to make it worthy as a national heritage.

Initially the first step towards the recognition of this had been the splendid gesture of the Acland family, who in 1944 had made over the whole of their Holnicote estate to the National Trust. This wonderful presentation embraced the whole of the Dunkery moorland from Porlock Vale to the bounds of the old forest, and included Horner Woods, Ley Hill, Selworthy Beacon and Winsford Hill. Since then the National Trust has striven to obtain still more land whenever possible, and has succeeded in acquiring the beautiful Watersmeet valley and the mighty cliffs of Heddon's Mouth and Woody Bay.

So now, with this we may close our story.

APPENDIX A

THE DOMESDAY MANORS OF THE EXMOOR COUNTRY

The manors of the hill country may be given as follows, starting from the country boundary in the north: Are (Oare), Chetenore (Kytnor or Culbone), Porloc (Porlock), Dovri (Doverhay), Winemeresham (Wilmersham), Stoche (Stoke Pero), Bagelie (Bagley), Hernola (Horner), Locumbe (Luccombe), Honicote (Holnicote), Hunecote (a part of Holnicote or else Huntscott), Wochetrew (Oaktrow), Udecombe (Cutcombe), Hauechewelle (Hawkwell—either near Cutcombe or Dulverton), Coarme (Quarme), Essetune (Exton), Winesford (Winsford), Aisseford (Exford—five parts or separate manors), Edmundesworthy (Almsworthy), Donescumba (Downscombe), Stone (Stone), Widepolle (Withypool), Ascwei (Ashway), Holne (Hollam), Broford (Broford), Dolvertone (Dulverton), Hauechewelle (Hawkwell), Anestinga (Anstey), Ringhendona (Ringcombe), Mollanda (Molland), Polham and Planteleia (Pulham and Praunsley), Nortmoltona (North Molton), Raordin (Radworthy), Braia (High Bray), Witefelda (Whitefield), Gretedona (Gratton), Walleurda (Wallover), Celdacumba (Challacombe), Radeuda (Radworthy in Swincombe), Witefelda (Whitefield north-west of Challacombe), Rodeliea (Rowley), Pearacomba (Parracombe), Lintona and Incrintona (Lynton and Ilkerton), Hantona (Caffins Heanton), Ciretona (Cheriton), Contesberia (Countisbury), Lina (East Lyn), Lancoma (Lank Combe), Bicheordin (Badgeworthy) and Brandona (Brendon).

Taking a look round at the Exmoor country as seen through Domesday Survey, we see Oare as a moderate-sized manor with land to six ploughs, six ploughs, seven villeins, five bordars, four serfs, two acres of meadow, fifteen acres of wood-land and pasture two leagues long. Culbone has land for two ploughs, two ploughs, two villeins, one bordar and one serf, fifty acres of pasture and a hundred acres of woodland. Wilmer-sham has land to five ploughs, only two ploughs, five villeins, three bardars, three serfs, two hundred acres of pasture and as much woodland. Stock Pero has land for two ploughs, one plough, two bordars, one serf, fifty acres of pasture and sixty acres of woodland. Bagley has but one plough and 'two bordars owning half a plough' and fifty acres of pasture and twelve of woodland. Cutcombe is a fairly large manor having land to fifteen ploughs, with nine ploughs, eighteen villeins, five bordars, six serfs, six swineherds, a mill (a corn-mill was some-thing of importance), six acres of meadow, pasture two leagues long and woodland one league long. In addition to this a part of the land of the manor is held by three knights, who have two ploughs, four villeins, six bordars, two acres of meadow, fourteen of woodland and pasture half a league long.

Stone, near Exford, has land for two ploughs, 'but it has been waste' (in other words it has 'gone down' and relapsed to moorland). Exford itself is divided into fine small separate manors, which have respectively land for two ploughs, with two half-ploughs (presumably two separate teams of four oxen), one bordar, one serf, ten acres of meadow, ten of pasture and ten of 'underwood'; land for one plough, with half a plough, one bordar, three acres of meadow, ten of pasture and two of woodland; land for one plough, with one plough and a half-plough, two bordars, three acres of meadow and ten of pasture; 'land for two oxen', with one villein and fifteen acres of pasture; and for half a plough, 'but it has been laid down to grass' (this last seems to be but a plot of ground).

Almsworthy has land to six ploughs, with four ploughs, six villeins, nine bordars, two serfs, eight acres of meadow, thirty of underwood and pasture two leagues long, and when re-ceived 'was altogether wasted'. (Almsworthy does not exist today, except in the name of a common, but must have been somewhere north of Exford, probably in the Pittsworthy valley.) Downscombe has land to one plough, with half a plough, one bordar, six acres of meadow, six of pasture and three of woodland. Withypool has land to four ploughs and 'it was held by three foresters, Dodo, Almer and Godric'. (This is the only instance in which there is any reference of any sort to the Forest of Exmoor.)

Winsford is a large manor, having land to sixty ploughs, with fifteen ploughs, thirty-eight villeins, eleven bordars, nine serfs, a mill, eight acres of meadow, forty of woodland and pasture four leagues long. There is also some added land equal to four ploughs, with three villeins and twenty-three bordars. Ashway has land to six ploughs, with three ploughs, eleven villeins, three bordars, two serfs, an acre of meadow, sixty of woodland and pasture one league long. Dulverton has land for eleven ploughs, with five and a half ploughs, seventeen villeins, six bordars, six serfs, three acres of meadow, pasture one league long and as much woodland. Added to this was some more land, equal to ten ploughs, with four ploughs, eight villeins, three acres of meadow, pasture half a league long and woodland one league long. Hawkwell has land to three ploughs, with three ploughs (or five—here the terms are peculiar), three villeins, four bordars and one serf. It is still held by Ulf the Englishman, and another, Ulmar, holds part of it.

Anstey consists of three small manors, corresponding no doubt to East and West Anstey, plus some other separate part, which had respectively three and a half ploughs, three villeins, six serfs, twenty acres of wood, one of meadow and pasture one league long; two ploughs, eight villeins, one bordar, two serfs and forty acres of wood and pasture half a league in length; six ploughs, seven villains, five bordars, seven serfs, one swineherd rendering six swine and 120 acres of wood, six of meadow and pasture one league long.

Molland is divided also into three, the manors being probably those later known as Molland Sarazen, Molland Botreaux and Molland Champson. The larger part, held by the king, has nineteen ploughs, thirty villeins, twenty bordars, ten serfs and fifteen acres of wood, twelve of meadow and pasture three leagues long. The other two parts have respectively two ploughs, three villeins, four bordars, two serfs, thirty acres of woodland and one and a half of meadow; and one serf and 'three oxen' (*III boves*), and twelve acres of wood and three of meadow.

Ringcombe is a small manor with but half a plough and two villeins.

Pulham and Praunsley are two small manors lumped together, having land to three ploughs, with one plough, one villein, two bordars and five acres of meadow and six of woodland.

North Molton, the largest of the moorland manors (if so it may be called), has land to one hundred ploughs, with forty-seven ploughs, forty-four villeins, fifty bordars, eleven serfs, fifteen swineherds, four farriers, two leagues of meadow, two leagues of pasture and one of coppice. The presence of four farriers—blacksmiths—argues that it was already something of a small township and centre of local industry.

Radworthy, either North or South, has land to three ploughs, with three ploughs, eight villeins, four serfs, one acre of meadow, forty of pasture and woodland one league long. Gratton has land to eight ploughs, with two ploughs, six villeins, three bordars, one serf, twelve acres of meadow, two hundred of pasture and thirty of woodland. High Bray has land to six ploughs, with four ploughs, six villeins, two bordars, one serf, thirty acres of meadow, twenty of wood and pasture two leagues in length. Whitefield, which goes with High Bray, has land for two ploughs, with one plough, two villeins, one bordar and ten acres of wood. Wallover does not specify ploughland: it just has one plough, four villeins, three bordars, one serf, sixty acres of pasture and fifty of wood. Challacombe has land to three ploughs, with a plough and a half, three villeins, two bordars, one serf, seven acres of meadow and ten of pasture. Radworthy (in Swincombe), has land to six ploughs, with one plough plus 'two plough oxen', three villeins, one serf, three acres of meadow, twenty of woodland and two leagues of pasture. Whitefield (near Challacombe) has land for two ploughs, 'it was waste' but now pays tax (presumably it has been reclaimed). Rowley has land for two ploughs, with one plough, three villeins, two bordars, one acre of meadow, thirty of pasture and ten of wood. Parracombe has six ploughs, five villeins, eight bordars, five serfs, thirty acres of wood, eight of meadow and one league of pasture. Caffins Heanton has land to three ploughs, with two ploughs, three villeins, two serfs, thirty acres of pasture and ten of wood. Cheriton has land for two ploughs, with two ploughs, four villeins, two bordars, two serfs, twenty acres of wood and two leagues of pasture.

Lynton and Ilkerton go together. Between them they have land to twelve ploughs, with twelve ploughs, thirteen villeins, one bordar, twelve serfs, pasture two leagues long and woodland of seven furlongs. Also here was a big herd of wild horses. Lyn, either West or East, has land to seven ploughs, with seven ploughs, nine villeins, five bordars, five serfs, two swineherds, a new mill, pasture two leagues in length and woodland half a league long. Countisbury has land to ten ploughs, with ten ploughs, twelve villeins, six bordars, fifteen serfs, one swineherd, two acres of meadow, fifty acres of wood and pasture one league in length.

Brendon we have already quoted in full. Lank Combe is just a little place with land to one plough and one villein there, and Badgeworthy is another small place (set in what is now called the Doone Valley), with land for two ploughs, and two ploughs, two villeins, one serf, five acres of meadow and thirty of pasture—'it was waste'.

APPENDIX B

EXMOOR PLACE-NAMES OF THE THIRTEENTH AND EARLY FOURTEENTH CENTURIES

Taking a look round at our hill country from Oare to Brendon about the time of the said year A.D. 1300, we find Ar (Oare), Bromsterte (Broomstreet), Kytenore (Kytnor-Culbone), Yarnor (Yarnor), La Putte (Pitt), Westcote (Westcott), Estkote (Eastcott), Berlanger (Birchanger), Porlock (Porlock), Dovery (Doverhay), Westloccombe (West Luccombe), Estloccombe (East Luccombe), Hunekote (Holnicote), Blakeford (Blackford near Holnicote or Blackford above Lucott), Hiernore (Horner), Holte (Holt), Leyewodecoke (Woodcock Ley), Bugedehole (Buckethole), Leucote (Lucott), Litlecombe (Littlecombe), Wynemersham (Wilmersham), Stokpiro (Stoke Pero), Cludesham (Cloutsham), Swetehegh (Sweetery), Bagel (Bagley), Hauekwill or Hauekeswelle (Hawkwell), Elleworthe (Elsworthy), Style (Stile), Forde (Ford), la Walles (Walland), la Stert or Sturte (Steart), Hanecumbe (Hannycombe), Nordecumbe (North Cumbe), Cumbeshered (Combeshead), Langeham (Langham), Waddene (Weddon), Coddesende (Codsend), Quarmenonceus (South, Quarme Moncereux), Beggesquarme (North or Begger Quarme), Exetone (Exton), Tettebroke (Edbrook), Wynesford (Winsford), Upcote (Upcott), Wydecombe (Withycombe), Nethercote (Nethercote), Asse (Ash), Combe (Combe—there are two in Exford), Exeford (Exford), Exfordemon (Exford Monachorum or Monkham), Scharrcote (Sharcott), Larvercombe (Larcombe), Almundesworthy (Almsworthy), Pittenewerthe (Pitsworthy), la Hylle in Almandeswerthe (Hill in Exford), Riscumbe (Riscombe), Chubbizete (Chibbet), le Schoyele (Showl in Exford) Wytepol or Wydipole (Withypool), la Langacre (Landacre), la Newlond (Newland in

Withypool or Exford), Hyldeweye (Hillway), la Blakelaund (Blackland), Brizteneworth (Brightworthy), Blackmore (Blackmoreland), Halsgreve or Haselgrove (Halsgrove), Foxtwichene (Foxtwitchen), Uppington (Uppington), Bradeleghe (Bradley), Cnaploc or Knapelok (Knaplock), Loscombe (Liscombe), Ashweye or Asseweye (Ashway), la Slade (Slade), Werth (Worth), Westaway (Westwater?), Hauekerigge (Hawkridge), la Sele (Zeal), Hindeham, (Hinam), Hordecumbe (Highercombe), Eastdraydon (East Draydon), Westdraydon (West Draydon). Broford (Broford), Mileshangre (Mousehanger), Halham (Hollam), Syderham (Siderham), la Hele (Hele), la Merse (Marsh), Dulvertone (Dulverton), Childecote (Chilcott), Tolchett (Cawkett), Hauekeswell (Hawkwell), Estanesty (East Anstey), Westanestige (West Anstey), Lillescombe (Liscombe), Wadcomb (Waddicombe), Donyslegh (Dunsley), Radenasse (Radnige), Churecombe (Cherricombe), Blakedon (Blackerton), Smalecumb (Smallacombe), Westwodeburn (Woodburn), Gopewell (Guphill), Wodelonde (Woodland), la Hull (Hill), Combe (Combe), Yoo (Yeo Mill), Brumelcombe (Brimblecombe), Bromlegh (Bremley), la Grutt (Gourt), Smalecumbe (Smallacombe), Lokiworthi (Luckworthy), Langcumbe (Landcombe) Lilleshull (Lyshwell), Stone (Stone), Poleworthi (Pulworthy or Pulsworthy), Leghe (Lee), Mollaund Chaumpeus (Chamson), la Hulle (Hill), Godecumbe (Gatcombe), Carswill (Kerswell), Bykencote (Bickingcott), Sundercumb (Sundercombe), Praunstesle (Praunsley), Radeworthi (Radworthy, North or South), Haseleg (North Heasley), Felleden (Fylden), Shortecomb (Shortacombe), Butterwurthe (Buttery), Bayntwitchen (Bentwitchen), la Hurde (West Yard), Kydeworth (Kedworthy), Mixenwurthi (Muxworthy), Littlcote (Lydcott), Fuleford (Fullaford), Nattesleye (Natesley), Whitefelde (Whitefield Barton near Challacombe), Radeweithe (Radworthy in Swincombe), Rughelegh (Rowley Barton), Heglegh (Highley), Brudewyk (Breadwick), Holdestan (Holdstone), Chymecote (Kemacott), Ketecote (Kittitoe),

Kynewalton (Killington), Trenlisho (Trentishoe), Mattynho (Martinhoe), Wellangre (Woolhanger), Hilcrinton (Ilkerton), Yanton (Caffins Heanton), Westlyn (West Lyn), Fershull (Furzehill), Thornworthy (Thornworthy), Stocke (Stock), Shortecomb (Shortacombe), Radespree (Ratsbury), Legh (Lee), la Clive (Cleve), Sperhangre (Sparhanger), Ashdene (Ashton), Combe (Combe), Doggeworth (Dogsworthy), Brandum (Brendon), Chirinton (Cheriton), Ferlee or Farlegh (Farley), Bikeweithe or Baggeheye (Badgeworthy or Badgery), Tibecote (Tippercott), Slocumb (Slocombeslade), Leoford (Leeford). And with this we are back to Oare again, where we began.

PLACE-LIST FROM THE PERAMBULATION OF
EXMOOR FOREST, 1298

The list begins with 'the lands between the bounds and the sea'—Yenworthy and Oare—and goes on with the 'vill' of Kytenore (Culbone) with woods, heaths and other appurtenances, the vill of Yernar (Yarnor) with woods, heaths, etc., the vill of Porlock with woods, heaths, etc., the vill of Bossington with woods, heaths, etc., the vill of Westloctun (West Luccombe) with woods, heaths, etc., the vill of Wyverssmerssham (Wilmersham) with woods, heaths, etc., the vills of D'Overey (Doverhay) and Est-loctut (East Luccombe) with woods, heaths, etc., the vills of Broggelesnole (Buckethole) and Leuecote (Lucott) with woods, heaths, etc., the wood called Worthe (Worthy) with heath, etc., the vill of Stoke (Stoke Pero) with woods, etc., the vill of Chittesham (Cloutsham?) with woods, heaths, etc., the vill of Honecetholne (Honicote?) and Broford with woods, heaths, etc., the hamlets of Forde and Style with the wood of Hau'combe (Hawkcombe) and the heath of Dunnerhay. The lands of Elleworthe (Ellsworthy) with woods and heaths, the vills of Hawkwelle and la Welles (Walland?) with woods, heaths, etc., the manor of Codecombe (Cutcombe) with woods, heaths, etc., the vill of Quarmunces

(Quarm Monceaux) with woods, heaths, etc., the vill of Almonesworth (Almsworthy) with woods, heaths, etc. The vill Exfordemony (Exford) with woods, heaths, etc., the vill of Beggar Quarme with woods, the vill of Wineforde (Winsford) with woods, heaths, etc., the hamlet of Wydecombe (Withycombe) with woods, heaths, etc., the hamlet of Hoo (Howe) with woods, heaths, etc., the hamlet of Tettebroke (Edbrook) with woods, heaths, etc., the vills of Exton, Hawkbrugge (Hawkridge) and Langacre (Landacre) with woods, heaths, etc., the vill of Widepole (Withypool) with woods, heaths, etc., the hamlet of Brutenesworthy (Brightworthy) with woods, heaths, etc., the hamlet of Westasway (West Ashway) with woods, heaths, etc., the hamlet of Loscumbe (Liscombe) with woods, heaths, etc., the hamlet of Eastashway with woods, heaths, etc., the hamlet of Telchete (Cawkett?) and la Merse (Marsh) with woods, heaths, etc., the vill of Dulvertone with woods, heaths, etc., the hamlet of Hawkwell with woods, etc., and the priory of Burlich (Barlynch) with woods, heaths, etc.

APPENDIX C

FREE SUITORS OF EXMOOR

The earliest list—that of 1797—gives the 'suits' as follows:

Ham, two; East Rew (Row), one; Wilskier, one; Kelskier, one; Holecombe (Hollowcombe), one; West Holecombe, one; Colland, one; Slade, one; Sayles (Zeal), two; Shortcombeland (Shircombe), two; Foxcombe, one; Huntercombly, one; South Batsham, one; North Batsham, one; Blackmoreland, one; South Hill, one; Kings, one; Waterhouse, one; Knighton, two; Brightonworthy, four; Landacre, four; Hillway, two; Blackland, three; Woolpitland, one; Halsgrave, one; Foxtwitchen, one; Witherslade, one; Sweetwalls, one; Upington, one; Garlicombe, one; Dodhays, one; Wayhouse, one; Broadmead-house, one; Gibbs, one; Hole, two; Newland, three.

A later list—indeed the final one, for it is taken from the Inclosure Award of 1819—gives a similar but slightly differing version:

Ham and Putsham, two; Huntercombe Ley, one; Foxcombe, one; Shorcombe, one; Wester Shorcombe, one; Wester Sayles (Zeal), one; Easter Sayles, one; Slade, one; West Hollowcombe, one; East Hollowcombe, one; East Rew, one; Kelshire or Colsher, one; Wilshier, one; Collands, one; Higher Lanacre, two; Lower Lanacre, two; Hillway, two; Hole or Hawlse, one; East Hole, one; Higher Blackland, two; Lower Blackland, one; Woolpit Land, one; Newland, three; Higher Brightworthy, one and a half; Middle Brightworthy, one and a half; Lower Brightworthy, one; Knighton, two; Waterhouse, one; Broadmead, one; Halsgrove, one; Weatherslade, one; Foxtwitchen, one; Dodhays, one; Gibbs, one; Garlicombe, one; Wayhouse, one; Sweetwalls, one; King's, one; Uppington, one; South Hill, one; Blackmoreland, one; North Batsham, one; South Batsham, one.

If one compares these two lists, it will be seen that the apparent discrepancy is due to a temporary amalgamation of neighbouring farms at one time or another. In this we have a clue to the odd or uneven distribution of suits. A half-suit would represent the lands of a defunct holding being divided between two other farms, and two suits would likewise indicate two original tenenments being put together permanently. Most probably this took place following the Black Death, when various small farms would have fallen empty and been abandoned. For practical purposes, since a suitor on horseback had to answer for each suit, the grouping of the first list is the most sensible—half a horseman would have been rather difficult to produce!

THE SUITORS-AT-LARGE

The 'townships' represented by Suitors-at-Large were those that bordered upon the forest, and for each a suitor, accompanied by from one to four 'hands', had to do suit at the Courts. The 'townships' were:

Oare, Yarnor and Kitnor, Almsworthy, Winsford Rivers, Ashway, Ashwick, Anstey Crewes, Anstey Reigny, Molland Botreaux, Molland Sarzen, North Molton, North Radworthy, South Radworthy, Whitechapple, High Bray, Charles, Challacombe Raleigh, Challacombe Regis, Wallworthy (Wallover), Parracombe, Lyn and Woolhanger, Lynton and Countisbury, Brendon.

The freeholders—or 'lords', as they are rather grandly called—were those of all the ancient manors or freeholds about the moor, and were supposed to attend at the Courts in person. These freeholds were:

Porlock, Oare; Yarnor and Kitnor; Colchett, Lucott and Buckethole; Woodcock's Ley; West Luccombe; East Luccombe, Wootton Courtney; Stoke Pero; Cutcombe Mohun; Cutcombe Raleigh; Thorn Bridge(?); Almsworthy; Withypool Ives; Withypool Sins; Langred (Landacre?); Ormond and Barkley(?); Halsgrove; Hillway; King's Land; South Hill; North Batsham; Ham; Foxcombe; Slade; Winsford Rivers; Winsford Boring; Winsford; Withycombe; Bradley; Ashway Ford; Ashway Mounsey; Ashway Ashwick; Hawkwell; Combe Reigny; Anstey Crewes; Anstey Reigny; Molland Sarazen; Molland Botreaux; Champson Molland; North Radworthy; South Radworthy; Whitechaple; Buckland; North Molton; Charles; Whitefield; High Bray; Gratton; Wallworthy; Challacombe Raleigh; Challacombe Regis; Parracombe; Martinhoe; Coffins Heanton; Lynton and Countisbury; Lyn and Woolhanger; Ratsbury and Sparhanger; North Fursehill; South Fursehill; Brendon.

APPENDIX D

SOME NOTABLE RUNS WITH THE NORTH DEVON STAGHOUNDS

On the morning of 3rd October 1781 a stag was found in Miller's Wood in the parish of Goodleigh. The pack was laid on at Chelfham Bridge, and from here they ran to Birchwood and on to Bratton Down. Thence the stag headed for the Forest, by Castlehead to the Barle, up over to Blackpits, then by Prayway to Warren. He turned for Larkbarrow, went out to Exford Common, crossed over by Alderman's Barrow for Lucott Moor, then went down by Poole Bridge to the Horner coverts. After running these big woods for nearly an hour he was brought to bay and killed at Eastwater Foot. From Goodleigh to Horner is twenty miles as the crow flies, and with turning and then doubling in covert hounds must have run many more.

In 1785 hounds found a stag in Longwood in the parish of North Molton and ran him to Horner Green. Though the point itself was not a very great one, being only twelve miles or so, the stag ran a twisting line, going by or around Darlick, Hawkridge, Lytton, Sheardon, Cow Castle, Simonsbath, Exe Head and on to the Chains, then to Hoaroak, Badgeworthy, Weirwood, Black Barrow, Alderman's Barrow, Lucott Moor and down to Horner Woods, where he ran the coverts until finally killed at Horner Green. The chronicler claims that this chase was over forty-five miles as hounds ran, and the time from lay-on to kill a little more than four hours.

The following year hounds ran a similar line in reverse, meeting at Horner and killing at Old Park, near North Molton, and the distance covered was probably not much less than the preceding. The quarry on this occasion was the Old Badgeworthy Stag, known to be at least twenty years old and carrying a head of nineteen points.

On 13th September 1804 a stag from Chargot Wood, near Luxborough, ran a twisting line over the Brendons to end at Highleigh Weir below Morebath, and here the chronicler claims that the chase was of at least fifty-five miles and run in five hours and forty minutes. He probably exaggerated, but certainly it would seem that this was one of the longest distances ever run by hounds.

One very fine run was that of 3rd October 1815, when hounds met at Cutcombe, and after tufting Oaktrow Wood, which was blank, roused a stag under Cloutsham. This stag took them to Langcombe Head, over Stoke Pero Common and Lucott Moor, on to Exford Common and to Larkbarrow, from there to Toms Hill and over Pinford Bog to Exe Cleeve. He then crossed out to Honeymead, and down to water at the Barle under Cow Castle, then up over Sheardon and on to the Fyledon Ridge and down through Darlick to Longwood; from there down to Heasley Mill, up over South Radworthy, down through the farther wood to the Mole. He ran on through North Molton, crossing the churchyard, then to Vennbottom to Rabscott and down to Brayley Bridge and on down to Castle Hill Park. Then to Northgate and through Lower Beer, to turn down through Winstead and Barton to Hudscott near Chittlehampton, and to Waterslake Brake. Here he was viewed, and raced down to Meathbridge and to Slatterleigh Marsh, where he was taken at last. Only seven riders out of a field of some two hundred were up at the finish. The stag himself proved to be a four-year-old. From Cloutsham to Slatterleigh Marsh is a distance of almost twenty miles as the crow flies, and as hounds run must have been quite double that. The chronicler does not this time venture any estimate of the length, but says this was one of the best and longest runs ever remembered.

Another fine run was that from the Barnstaple Fair meet in 1819. A stag harboured in Tidecombe at length broke up over

Thorn, and took hounds over Bratton Down to Leeworthy Post and down to water. After a check, hounds were lifted to a view on Shoulsbarrow (it seems doubtful if this were to the original stag), and ran on over to the Barle and up Whiteladders to Simonsbath. The stag then turned by Cloven Rocks and by Honeymead to Cow Castle, and from thence beat down to Sheardon Hutch and Landacre Bridge. He turned out over Withypool Common to Lytton and down to Willingford, then up to White Post and on to the Molland enclosures, then back to Lyshwell and down the Danesbrook to Hawkridge South Wood, then up Whiterocks to Buckminster, down to the Barle and over to Mounsey Castle, down to the river again under Ashway and then down the water to Marsh Bridge, where he was taken. The point from Tidecombe to Marsh Bridge is eighteen miles, and there must have been much turning and doubling, making the whole run of great length. Of the five hundred horsemen who rode from the meet that morning, the number who saw the finish must have been very small, though just how many is not recorded.

Another eighteen-mile point was made by hounds on 16th May 1820, but this was from Huntsham, below the Brendons, to Bycott near Chumleigh in mid Devon, and was over a line of country south of the moor. The chase was run through the parishes of Huntsham, Tiverton, Stoodleigh, Bampton, Oakford, Brushford, East Anstey, Knowstone, Rose Ash, Meshaw and Chumleigh, and lasted three and a half hours. The recorder claims that the distance was thirty miles from point to point, which of course it was not, but he probably meant as hounds ran. The quarry was a spring hind, presumably a barren one.

Though few days could equal the preceding for length of point, many were the good long moorland runs that were had in the last years of the old pack. As, for instance, 15th August 1820, when the hounds met at Twitching (Titchen farm—now a ruin), near Culbone, to open the season. Having tufted the cliff woods and found them blank, a move was made to Home-bush, and eventually a stag was roused in Parkwood. The pack was laid on at Parson's Hill and ran through Hawkcombe to Horner Wood over Cloutsham Ball to Sweetery, on by Lang-combe Head to Chetsford Water, and by Alderman's Barrow for the forest. The deer ran Longcombe, went over to the Exe, crossing below Warren, on across Honeymead and came to water below Cow Castle. He broke up over Ferny Ball for Sandy-way and Darlick, and so to Longwood; thence to Barham and Span, where they fresh-found him, and raced him over Shortacombe and Whitefield and to Liddicot, to bring him to bay in the water above Brayford.

On the 29th of the same month hounds met at Bratton, and the tufters found in Riddlewood. The pack were laid on at Bulton Bridge and ran their stag through Tidecombe to Thornbrake, up over Westland Pound, over Rowley Down, on to Hoaroak and down to Hillsford Bridges; then on for Brendon and to Badgery Wood, over to Chalk Water and up to Black Barrow, over to Chetsford Water and to Nutscale Brake, and on over the hill to Sweetery. From there the deer turned back over Cloutsham Ball, down to Eastwater Foot and down the water to Horner Green, then over the hill into Hawkcombe, up over the common to Weirwood, down the water to Oareford, then up over to Titchen and Silcombe, and to Culbone, where they took him at last. Says the commentator: 'This was a very arduous day. The chase lasted seven hours and a half.'

On 10th October 1821 the meet was at Buryhill and the tufters found in Haddon. The stag broke for the Exe and, with the pack laid on, went by Baronsdown, Stockham Wood and Chilly Bridge to Court Down and by Ballneck to Marsh Wood; thence up the Barle and up over Hawkridge Ridge to South Wood, back over the Ridge again, up the river to South Barton Wood, up Huntercombe and over to Lyshill, up the Willingford water to Lyttons and Sandyway and down to Sherdonford. From here the stag beat up the water to Kinsford, then turned back and was taken at Emmets under Redway. This great chase was run in two and a quarter hours.

Another fine chase was from Bray on 29th August 1823. The stag, roused in the Bray coverts, ran by Emmetts, Cornham Brake and Duredown to Prayway, then turned down across the Exe, up over Honeymead and to water at Cow Castle. Then to Sherdon Hutch, over Withypool Common to Lyshill, then to West Anstey Common back to the Danesbrook, up over East Anstey Common and to Vennford. After some difficult hunting he was finally taken at Hawkwell in the parish of Dulverton.

APPENDIX E

ENCLOSURE OF EXMOOR COMMONS

These wholesale enclosures proceeded as follows:

Bratton Down and Berry Hill (Bratton Fleming), 1841. Almsworthy Common (Exford), 1848. Stoke Ridge (Stoke Pero), 1850. Ison (Winsford), 1851. Winsford, otherwise Staddon (Winsford), 1852. Exford South or Munckham Common (Exford), 1852. Dulverton North Moor or Streamcombe (Dulverton), 1852. Eastern and Western Commons (North Molton), 1853. North Hey, North Radworthy Common, Heady Park and Shortacombe (North Molton), 1853. Span Common (North Molton), 1853. Blindwell and Worth Common (Twitchen), 1853. Twitchen Common (Twitchen), 1853. East Anstey Common (East Anstey), 1856. Hawkridge Manor (Hawkridge), 1859. Lyn Down and Lyn Cleave (Lynton), 1860. The Outer Down, the In Down, and the Valley of Rocks (Lynton), 1860. Parracombe Common (Parracombe), 1862. Oare Common (Oare), 1863. Porlock Common (Porlock), 1867. Shoulsbarrow Castle Common (High Bray), 1872. Wootton Courtenay Manor (Wootton Courtenay), 1872.

BIBLIOGRAPHY

J. Billingsley, *General View of the Agriculture of the County of Somerset*, 1798.

C. P. Collyns, *Notes on the Chase of the Wild Deer in the Counties of Devon and Somerset*, 1862, 1902.

Devonshire Association, *The Devonshire Domesday and Geld Inquest*, 1884–1892.

Earl Fortescue, *Records of the North Devon Staghounds, 1812–1818*, 1887.

E. J. Rawle, *Annals of the Ancient Royal Forest of Exmoor*, 1893.

W. H. P. Greswell, *The Forests and Deer Parks of the County of Somerset*, 1905.

Victoria County Histories of Devon and Somerset, 1906.

E. T. MacDermot, *History of the Forest of Exmoor*, 1911.

J. S. Hill, *Place-names of Somerset*, 1913.

C. S. Orwin, *The Reclamation of Exmoor Forest*, 1929.

J. E. B. Gover, *Place-names of Devon*, 1932.

Also: Ordnance Survey Sheets 163, North Devon (Barnstaple) and 164, West Somerset (Minehead).

Transactions of the Devonshire Association (numerous volumes).

Proceedings of the Somerset Archaeological and Natural History Society (numerous volumes).